ENTOMBED

My True Story:
How Forty-five Jews Lived Underground
and Survived the Holocaust

Bernard Mayer

Aleric Press

All of the events portrayed in this book are true
and the people are real. Several names have been
changed.

Third printing. Cover design by Martin Silverman
Cover photo: The author, Bernard Mayer, at the age
of 14. The photo was taken in the labor camp in
Drohobycz, Poland.

Library of Congress Cataloging in Publication Data
Mayer, Bernard
Entombed: My True Story: How Forty-five Jews
Lived Underground and Survived the Holocaust

Library of Congress number: 94-71465
ISBN: 0-9641508-0-8

This book is dedicated to

my mother, TONIA MAYER,

and to

my brother, JAKOB MAYER.

None of the forty-five lives

would have been saved

without their courage, foresight,

and perseverance.

Acknowledgments

My deep appreciation and gratitude go to my friends and family, without whose help this book would not have been possible. I want to thank Rubin Pannor for his invaluable ideas.

I am deeply grateful to my sons Alan and Eric for their continued interest and help in editing the manuscript. Thanks to my friend Betsy Kaplan for her encouragement and support. And special thanks to Irving Lieber, whose memory of events and dates was most helpful. I also want to thank Phyllis Goldenberg, my editor, who made me write at times when I was emotionally exhausted and wanted to quit. She was available to me at all times and lived through the events with me.

Many thanks to Martin Silverman for designing the cover and title page and to Jim Hunter for sketching the house and the bunker.

Contents

Author's Note

The Jews, who lived in the Middle East in an area presently known as Israel, have a four thousand year history started by Abraham. Approximately two thousand years ago, they were exiled from their homeland by the Romans and dispersed throughout Europe and North Africa. They were tradesmen, tenant farmers, merchants, and professionals.

Throughout the years the Jews were expelled from many countries including England in the year 1215, France in 1306, and Spain in 1492. Over a four hundred year period, the largest population of Jews were concentrated in Eastern Europe including Poland and Russia. They were always a persecuted and ridiculed people because of their religion.

At the time of the Holocaust, the Jews were a minority in every country. Six million were killed, among them were one and one-half million children. The Holocaust was a culmination of thousands of years of persecution and discrimination.

B.M.

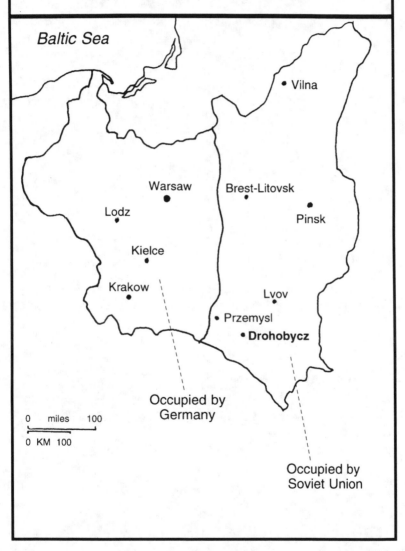

Poland June 22, 1941
Occupied and divided by Germany and The Soviet Union

Baltic Sea

• Vilna

Warsaw
•

Brest-Litovsk
•

Lodz
•

Pinsk
•

Kielce
•

Krakow
•

Lvov
•

• Przemysl

• **Drohobycz**

Occupied by Germany

0   miles   100

0   KM   100

Occupied by Soviet Union

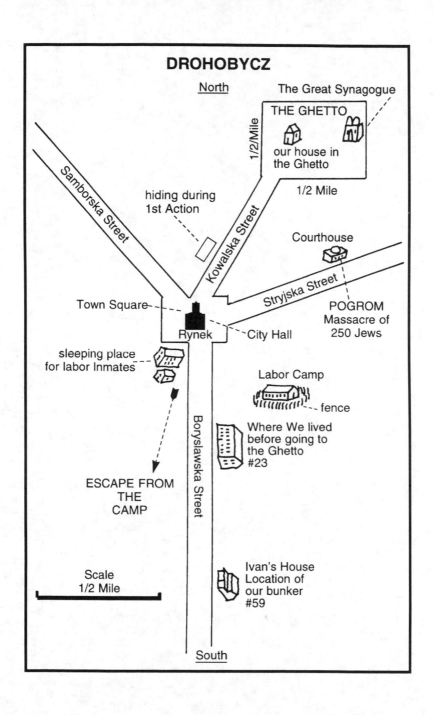

DROHOBYCZ

North

The Great Synagogue

THE GHETTO

our house in the Ghetto

1/2 Mile

1/2 Mile

Samborska Street

Kowalska Street

hiding during 1st Action

Courthouse

Stryjska Street

Town Square

Rynek

City Hall

POGROM Massacre of 250 Jews

sleeping place for labor Inmates

Labor Camp

fence

Boryslawska Street

Where We lived before going to the Ghetto #23

ESCAPE FROM THE CAMP

Scale 1/2 Mile

Ivan's House Location of our bunker #59

South

Bernard Mayer (author) on vacation with his
mother and father in 1935.

Szymon, Jakob, and Clara in 1922.
Sister Clara and Brother Szymon were killed.

Cousin Helen, a medical student at the
University of Lvov before the Nazis arrived,
was killed in June 1943 in the labor camp.

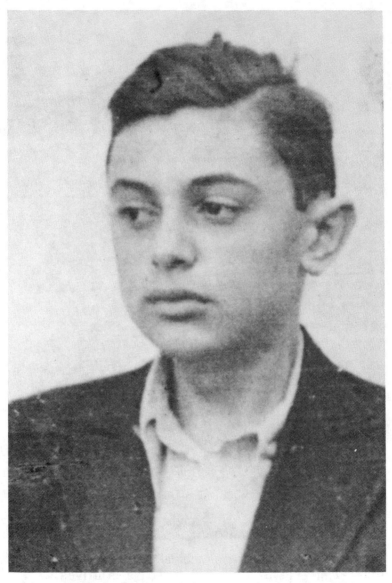

Bernard Mayer in the labor camp at the age of 14

Foreword

Before World War II, the town of Drohobycz where I was born, was located in eastern Poland. Now it is in the Ukraine. Though national borders have changed frequently, the town itself remains where it always stood--in hilly country surrounded by forests and farms, about 120 kilometers south of the city of Lvov.

Drohobycz was founded in 1092, and Jews lived there since the fifteenth century. When the German army arrived in Drohobycz, on June 29, 1941, 50,000 people lived in town. About 17,000 of them were Jews, 18,000 Ukrainians, and 15,000 Poles. The Jews were mostly artisans, professionals, and former merchants working for the Soviet government.

We had a well-integrated community before the war. Some apartment buildings had only Gentiles or Jews, but all over town many apartments and duplex homes were occupied by both Jews and Gentiles.

My father Isaac was born on a farm in the Carpathian mountains about fifty kilometers from Drohobycz. He came from a family of 13 children. As a boy, he and his brothers walked ten kilometers each way to school. As an adult, he was short, stocky, with black hair and blue eyes. He was bright. Although most of his brothers and sisters emigrated to America, he remained in Drohobycz because of his success in business.

In 1908 Isaac married into a prominent Jewish family in Drohobycz. At the turn of the century, when oil was discovered in the area, my father bought and sold oil shares and became prosperous. He also was a cattle importer. He and his wife Esther had three children--Szymon, Clara, and Jakob. In 1920 Esther died of tuberculosis, leaving Isaac with their three young children.

Four years later Isaac met and married Tonia Gelber, who was eighteen years younger than he. She was a caring woman for him and his three children, who were eight, ten, and twelve years old. She became their stepmother at a youthful age and soon was efficiently motherly. She told me that she had married my father because of his kind blue eyes.

In 1928 I was born to Isaac and Tonia, and they named me Bezio. Tonia, aided by maids, ran a full household in our house next to a monastery, where we lived until I was six. The monastery and the Gentile neighborhood showed me different life styles. I watched the nuns doing their chores. When my father got sick, the nuns would come to bring him medications. My mother took care of me and her three stepchildren, who loved her as their own mother.

During my early years, I was a quiet child. I got a lot of attention from my brother Jakob, who protected me in every way. Because I was small, my sister Clara always watched out that I shouldn't get hit by other children. But my oldest brother Szymon kept away from me. He was always busy with his friends and girls.

In 1937 when I was nine, my father died. Although he had suffered from high blood pressure for many years, not until the last few years of his life did he slow down in business. Weak and ill, knowing he would die soon, he helped my mother open a chocolate store. And after my father died, it was my mother's chocolate store that kept the family together.

In 1939 borders changed again when Hitler and Stalin made a pact that split Poland. Germany occupied the western part, and Russia the eastern part. The Russians took over our area, and Drohobycz became part of Russia. The Russians prohibited citizens from owning private businesses, and so the chocolate store came to an end.

On June 22, 1941, the Germans invaded the Soviet Union and within seven days they occupied our town. At the time of the German invasion, my mother was 41. She had fair skin, black hair, and was of medium height.

She was a gallant woman, who had overcome many disasters in her life. Among them was her escape from her home town of Tarnopol with her mother and sick brother during World War I. Wandering throughout Austria and Czechoslovakia from age 15 to 19, she supported herself by sewing garments. After the war she came to Drohobycz, where her sister lived and where she met Isaac.

At the time of the German invasion, my mother worked in a coffee factory packing the imitation coffee that was sold as coffee in those days.

My sister Clara was 26. She was pretty, petite, with black hair and black eyes. She was very close to my mother and used to help in the household chores. Like most Jewish girls in those days, Clara was waiting for a matchmaker to introduce her to a man she would marry. But during the Soviet occupation, the old traditions changed, and girls ventured to meet boys on their own. Eventually, Clara met her boyfriend, the butcher.

My brother Jakob was 24. He had black hair and blue eyes. Jakob was muscular, intelligent, and aggressive. He started working in a grocery store at the age of 15 and eventually became an expert coffee roaster and manager of the state-owned Soviet coffee factory. I considered Jakob the head of our household; he was my "father."

I was thirteen and small for my age. Life for me was happy. I played the mandolin, joined a string orchestra and the school choir. Reading was my hobby, and I enjoyed my schoolwork. When the war began, I had just finished the seventh grade. I was planning to become an accountant because the opportunities were good and I didn't want to do manual labor. To attend college, I would have had to leave town, which my family couldn't afford.

My oldest brother Szymon didn't live with us. Szymon, the handsomest of all of Isaac's children, was tall with black curly hair and a small mustache. On New Year's eve of 1935, I watched Szymon put on a tuxedo and stand in front of the mirror admiring himself. My father walked over to him and asked, "Where are you going so dressed up?"

"I'm going to a New Year's eve party," Szymon replied.

My father became furious and screamed, "A Jewish boy should go to a Christian party and dance with *shiksas* (non-Jewish girls)? This has got to end! I'll see Zalman, the matchmaker, and you'll be married soon. The entire town will now talk that Isaac Mayer's son dances with *shiksas*!"

Within a few months Szymon was engaged to a nice Jewish girl from the nearby town of Stryj. He saw her only three times before we all traveled to Stryj for Szymon's wedding. When the war began, Szymon was 29 and lived with his wife and two children in Stryj.

This is the story of my family and the Jews of Drohobycz.

The Pogrom

June 21, 1941

That Saturday night a performance by magicians was on my mind. I had just finished the seventh grade, and it was vacation time. After difficult tests, I felt relieved so I decided to venture alone, as I always did, to the new national theater to see the magicians. Only last week I had seen a performance of "Teveye Molocznyk" (Teveye the Milkman) in Ukrainian performed by the Drohobycz Repertory Theater. (Twenty-five years later it became a hit Broadway musical, "Fiddler on the Roof.")

I enjoyed the magicians' performance immensely, especially the disappearance of a diamond ring that belonged to a woman in the audience. The ring was eventually found in a large box, containing fifteen smaller boxes, hidden in the balcony.

The night was clear with the moon shining. I walked home alone, happy, content, admiring the beautiful evening. I thought with pleasure of the long summer weeks of just loafing around, not studying, being with my friends. When I opened the door, my mother greeted me with a surprise. "Bezio," she said, "tomorrow we are going on a picnic with Aunt Sala and the family." "That's great, I must go to sleep now, to get up early ," I said and entered my room.

June 22, 1941

Sunday early in the morning voices outside woke us. "A war is on! The Germans have attacked us!" I put on the radio and found that all Russian stations repeated the same news: the Germany army had crossed our borders and was advancing eastward.

My older brother Jakob was away on vacation in a resort near Lvov. My mother, sister, and I left our home to see my aunt down the street. We needed to talk about what preparations to make. My aunt Sala lamented that her daughter Helen was in Lvov in medical school. Helen would have difficulty coming home because all public transportation had been taken over by the Russian army.

During the next several days, chaos prevailed in town. Since we lived only 80 kilometers from the border, we expected the Germans to occupy our town within days.

Jakob came home three days later. He had been called to the Russian army while he was gone, but when he went to the induction center, no one was there any more. Some people in our building talked about escaping with the Russians, but only a few young boys decided to move out with them. No families in our building left.

The dusty Boryslawska Street where we lived was busy with wagons, horses, and trucks full of soldiers and civilians. I stood in front of my building looking at the rows of vehicles moving eastward.

June 29-30, 1941
I woke up early, dressed, and quietly opened the door and slipped into the dark hallway. Everyone in the house was still asleep. I found a lot of trash on the steps. Early summer daylight shone through the large glass front doors to the street. It was completely quiet outside, and the street was empty.

I wiped the glass windows with my shirt sleeve to be able to see outside. I was careful to stay inside. Then I saw two Red army sholdiers galloping on horses toward the center of town. I opened the door and watched them disappear behind clouds of dust. These were the last two Russian soldiers to leave Drohobycz, Poland.

The German army marched into town that same day. There was a very sad mood in our house, a three-story red brick apartment building built by Mr. Kupferman.

Gregory, our Ukrainian superintendent, closed the main gate into the courtyard of the building. Gregory was a short, stocky man, a chain smoker with dark hair combed to the side. His job was to wash the hallways and steps, and to sweep the courtyard, especially at the garbage bin. He and his wife lived in a small apartment at the gate to the courtyard.

We lived four blocks from the center of town at 23 Boryslawska Street. Seventeen Jewish families lived in the one- and two-bedroom apartments. We had running water and gas, and on each floor there were toilets shared by all the tenants.

Many apartments faced the courtyard because the building was U-shaped. The second and third floors had balconies all around, and in the afternoons or evenings, many of us would sit on the balconies facing each other and talk. Behind the building was an empty field where we kids congregated. We played football, or lay in the sunshine, sometimes to read a book. We had pear, apple, and cherry trees there.

My mother, Clara, Jakob, and I lived in a two-bedroom apartment on the second floor, facing the courtyard.

Our neighbors were the Feingolds. Mr. Feingold was thin, refined-looking, an educator who was director of the reformed (progressive) Hebrew school. This Hebrew school was not religious. People sent their kids there to learn the Hebrew language. There were no Conservative or Reform movements in our town.

Mrs. Feingold was a plump lady who suffered from depression. Their older daughter was eighteen, a very well behaved, pretty girl and a gymnasium graduate. Their younger daughter was fourteen and attended school with me. Mrs. Feingold would frequently come to our house and talk to my mother, who was a very good listener.

On the day the Russians left and the Germans arrived, Mrs. Feingold was visiting my mother. Whenever Mrs. Feingold didn't feel well, she had a flushed face. I recognized immediately that she needed to talk to my mother. She sat at the kitchen table, and my mother left her kitchen chores to join her. I heard Mrs. Feingold say, "You know, Tonia, I have a feeling that we should have left with the Russians. We may be in a lot of trouble here. My husband heard on the radio that the Germans are destroying the Jewish community in the Warsaw Ghetto."

My mother shook her head, "I couldn't see myself leaving my home."

June 30th

The next day early in the afternoon, all of us with apartments facing the courtyard heard Gregory's voice screaming, "Everyone hide in the attic! They are looking for Jews!"

None of us had been aware of the dangerous situation in town. We hurried to knock at the doors of those who lived facing the street to alert them to danger.

At first we didn't know who was looking for Jews. But half an hour later, a Jewish woman ran into our house telling us that the Ukrainians were picking up Jews and killing them. "It's a massacre," she sobbed. "Ukrainian peasants came to the courthouse. They stood all along the Stryjska Street leading to the courthouse with clubs, picks, knives, hammers. Gangs of young Ukrainians are roaming the Rynek (town square) picking up any Jew they can find and dragging them to the courthouse. There they club them and stab them to death. Please," she begged, "I want to hide with you." What she was describing was a totally new experience for us in Drohobycz. No one could believe that it could be true.

By now everyone had come out of their apartments and had gathered in the courtyard. We were not sure if the attic was the safest place to hide. They could easily find us because there were no doors to the attic. We had to weigh our options, but at the end there was only one choice.

Gregory looked at us with anxious eyes. He knew there was danger to all of us. Urgently he repeated, "All of you go to the attic. I see a mob coming in our direction. Hurry, go fast." His voice trembled with fear and anger. "I'm closing the gate, and I'm going to confront them. They will not enter this building!"

We all ran to the attic and sat down on the floor, which was coated with thick dust. The attic was huge-- covering the entire building--and filled with clotheslines. It was here that the tenants hung their laundry to dry. Walking around, you had to bend down constantly to avoid the clotheslines. Every tenant had washing tubs and scrub boards stored there, scattered all over the attic. The attic had no ventilation, and the heat from the tin roof engulfed us. It was difficult to breathe. We sat in family groups, in the darkest areas, hoping not to be noticed in case they should come for us.

My thoughts ran wild. Only a few days ago I was in the large theater watching the magician, the pianist, and the orchestra. Now I'm in the attic scared for my life. It was totally unreal.

It was completely quiet; no one uttered a word. We waited for about an hour.

Then we heard noises outside. A gang of about ten Ukrainian peasants approached our building, shouting, "Here are Jews! We know this building has a lot of Jews! Let's get them!"

My heart was beating fast. I looked at my mother, who was pale, almost fainting. She held my hand. I was scared that we might die.

We heard Gregory open the gate and close it. Then we heard his angry voice. "You are not coming into this building. I'm in charge here. First you have to kill me. You see I have this iron bar. I will kill one of you first."

"You're a Jew lover!" the crowd screamed. One of the peasants shouted above the others, "OK, we will leave now, but we will get even with you later."

Then we heard them leave. We felt relieved. My mother's face smiled at me, but her eyes were very sad. Gregory stood at the gate for half an hour more. When he came up to the attic, he told us, "You can come down now. The murderers have gone."

Gregory saved our lives that day. Later we realized that going to the attic or staying in our apartments would have made no difference; they would have found us either way. Gregory's heroic stance was the reason for our survival. He could have opened the gates, cooperated with the gang, and led them into the attic, which many Ukrainians would have done. Or he could have opened the gates and stood by when the gang ransacked the building and eventually found us. But Gregory had a conscience. He chose to stand up to the gang, taking a chance that he could have been killed. He protected us in the first onslaught on our lives. We all were overwhelmed by his heroic action.

The pogrom came as a surprise to us. In our town there was no murder or hate that I could remember, and especially such vicious anger at the Jews.

When we got back to our apartment, my mother shook her head and said, "We should have escaped with the Russians, my children. I have made a mistake."

Jakob tried to reassure her, "Mom, please be patient. In a few days the Red Army will be back and chase these Germans all the way into Germany. In a few days the Russians will liberate us."

Clara was terribly upset and looked very frightened. I sat in the corner of the kitchen and listened to them talk. I knew that the Russians would not return-- Jakob was just trying to cheer us up. I felt angry and trapped. We have to stick together, I thought. My dreams of continuing school were shattered.

July 1, 1941

The next day my mother and I ventured into town to find out what had happened to the rest of our family. We followed others, who knew that the pogrom was over. We went to see Aunt Lipcia and her husband Chaim, who lived in the Rynek.

We found my uncle in bed with a bandaged head. My aunt grabbed onto my mother and started to cry. "You should only know what happened to us," she sobbed. "We were having lunch when a large group of Ukrainians pounded on our door, and when we wouldn't open it, they broke down the door. They dragged us into the street to the courthouse. All along the way they beat us and kicked us. When we got to the courthouse, we saw a group of young men beating Jews mercilessly. Chaim was screaming to them, 'Don't hit my wife, hit me instead.' They hit him over the head many times, and he was bleeding all over. Eventually, I dragged him away and took him home. We found a doctor, who came and bandaged his head. He is very sick. We found many people dead and dying in the courtyard of the courthouse."

Then Aunt Lipcia explained what had caused the pogrom. "When the Ukrainians dragged us to the courthouse, they took us to see twelve or so dead bodies of Ukrainian prisoners. They had been killed by the Russian secret police before they left town. So the Ukrainians screamed at us that we were Communists and dirty Jews. That's why they were killing the Jews."

The day after our visit to Aunt Lipcia, I ventured on Stryjska Street toward the courthouse. As I walked, I looked at the sidewalk. All along I saw bloodstains. When I arrived at the courthouse, the gates were closed. Next door stood a beautiful Ukrainian church. Parishioners were just leaving the church, followed by the priest. I looked very sternly at the priest, thinking, "How could you have witnessed this massacre and not intervened?"

He noticed me, turned to me and said, "What are you doing here, Jew? Go home." I knew then that the church was not a friend of mine.

The Jews were the scapegoats for the Ukrainians' frustration. The Germans allowed the Ukrainians just one day for their pogrom, and then the Germans restored their own kind of order. During that one-day pogrom on June 30, 1941, more than 200 Jews in Drohobycz were murdered.

My uncle suffered for three months, lost his speech, became paralyzed, and died.

It was the beginning of our tragedy that liquidated the Jewish community in Drohobycz.

The White Armband

At the beginning of July, Jakob began working at a German warehouse. Every morning before work he had to go to the Judenrat in the old section of town to register for the job. The Judenrat office had a Jewish committee and leaders, whom the Germans dealt with about Jewish matters. At the end of the day, Jakob was given a half a loaf of bread for his work.

After a couple of days he came home very upset. He told us as soon as he walked in the door. "At the Judenrat they told me that starting Monday we all must wear a white armband with a star of David on our right arm. We must wear it at all times. Whoever will be found not wearing it will be shot on the spot."

"Oh, *Gottenyu*! (my God)" my mother cried. "What will happen next to us?"

"That's not all," Jakob looked at me. "On the bulletin board is a notice that says Jews may not attend any schools or enter libraries." His voice was serious. I knew this wasn't a joke, but I couldn't believe it.

"Jakob, it means that I can't continue my education. What am I going to do? I must go to school."

Jakob looked at me sternly and said, "Look, all of you.
You need to understand that we Jews will now be different
from everyone in town. The notice reads that we must
surrender our jewelry, radio, even furs. We can't leave the
house after 6 P.M., and we can't attend movies. And
everyone must work without pay."

I protested, "You mean that I must remove the
kangaroo fur collar from my coat?"

My mother and sister understood and accepted better
than I did. Immediately they started to sew white armbands
for all of us. They took blue thread and embroidered the star
of David on each armband. It seemed to me, as I watched,
that they were taking care to make the armbands look good.
How can it be, I thought? These terrible armbands and they
care to make them attractive.

I changed very quickly after that. I realized that we
Jews were no longer equals in our community, and I helped
my family find food by selling some of our clothing.

A couple of days later I put my armband on my right
arm. I asked my mother to take the fur collar off my coat,
and I took our radio to the German depot.

During that summer and fall, the Jewish leaders
organized labor camps. In these factories Jews worked
without pay, producing goods and materials for the
Germans. The idea was to satisfy the Germans so they
would keep the Jewish population of Drohobycz intact. The
leaders of the Judenrat assured the Gestapo officers in
charge of the Jews that we would be a benefit to them.

Since Drohobycz had three oil refineries and a skilled Jewish labor force, labor camps started in the city and its outskirts. The camps were called Herawka, Beskiden, Dachuvczarnia, Jana, and Statishe Werkstaten. Besides these camps, scores of Jews worked at the Germans' offices and houses repairing things, cleaning, and washing horses.

My sister Clara worked at the Gartnerei, the plant nursery. Her work was hard. She would come home tired and say to us, "I'm frightened working in this nursery. The Germans walk around all the time screaming at everyone."

"Maybe you can change jobs?" I asked her.

"That's not easy, Bezio," she smiled sadly. "You must have a permit from the German officer to change jobs."

November 21, 1941

The Germans gave the order for all Jews with disabilities to come to the staging area. Anyone with a doctor's note would be excused from labor. They were given several days notice--time enough to get a doctor's note. Like all German orders, this announcement came from the Judenrat. Two hundred and fifty men showed up at the staging area that morning. Some were disabled and crippled, but many were healthy men who wanted to avoid heavy labor. Among those who came with doctors' notices was Lonek Kestenberg, a handsome seventeen-year-old from our building. Lonek's father, Mr. Kestenberg was not well and had decided to get a doctor's notice. Since he had to deliver it early in the morning, his youngest son Lonek volunteered to go in his father's place. Lonek never returned.

Later we found out that all the people who had appeared at the staging area were immediately surrounded by Nazi soldiers, put on trucks, and taken to Bronica Ravine, five kilometers from Drohobycz, where they were shot.

The tragedy for Lonek's parents and his two brothers had an enormous effect on the residents of our building. All of us felt their tragic loss--especially me. Lonek had been my idol. He had taught me how to play football and had encouraged me to read books by taking me frequently to the library. I was terribly upset---never to see Lonek again? I couldn't believe it. He was young, I thought, and he had just been alive, like me. "I can't be without Lonek," I told my mother. "Who will take me to the football matches and to the library?"

Our family and all of the other Jews had two problems: feeding ourselves and keeping warm in the winter. Most of us worked but earned no wages. How does one eat? It was not a question of clothing, entertainment, or education, but just enough food to be able to work and survive. Those of us who had clothing or household items bartered with the peasants for food (usually potatoes, flour, grain). Most of us walked the streets with clothing or household items to trade for food. But there were many poor Jews who had nothing to trade. They were the first to die of hunger, disease, and cold.

The shoemaker's family was typical. They lived in the basement of our building facing the courtyard in one room that contained two beds, a stove, and a table. In front was the shoemaker's shop. The shoemaker was a bearded, religious man; his wife was small and frail. Before the Germans came, father and son worked together fixing shoes, eking out a meager living. The mother shopped and cooked. The son was in his twenties, dark-haired. He stayed indoors most of the time, but on Saturdays he would venture out in his Sabbath clothing and shiny shoes. He talked to me at times, usually smiling, asking me how I was doing in school.

When the Germans came, the shoemaker's family suffered immediately because they had no resources--no clothing or other items to barter for food. They were starving. The mother would go into the backyard, collect leaves, and cook them. That winter the shoemaker's son died of hunger, and a few months later the old couple were taken away in the first action.

All over town hundreds of people died of hunger. Our neighbors the Rosenbergs and their two children were not able to survive. They were poor before the Germans came, and afterward there was not enough food to keep them alive. The family grew pale, skinny, and sick. Mr. Rosenberg got a swollen belly because he filled up with potatoes and water. Walking through the streets in the morning, I saw dead Jews--old and young--lying against the walls of the buildings.

A couple of weeks after the Germans arrived, my brother Jakob went to the coffee factory where he had been manager. There he found Mr. Kobyla, a Ukrainian who had been made director of the place. Jakob told him that he was an expert coffee roaster and that he knew all about the factory. Mr. Kobyla told Jakob to start the factory, and they roasted imitation coffee made from oats and other grains, since real coffee was not available. Many sacks of grain filled the factory.

One day Jakob approached Mr. Kobyla. "I can save a few pounds of grain at each roasting," he proposed. "We can do it by wetting the roasted grain so it weighs more. Then we tell the Germans that the roasting process reduces the weight of the grain by five pounds more than it really does. This way we can save many pounds of grain and sell it on the black market." Grain was very much in demand.

Jakob struck a deal with Mr. Kobyla: they would split the proceeds between them--25 percent to Jakob, 75 percent to Kobyla. Each day Jakob sold two sacks of grain, and Kobyla and he pocketed the money. Mr. Kobyla was a passive partner. He figured that in case the Germans would find out about the scheme, they would catch the Jew, who was doomed anyway.

We were lucky. Now we had grain for food. We had the grain ground, and my mother baked bread and cooked the grain. We traded grain for potatoes, meat, and other food items. Under the Germans' new laws, Jews were not allowed to slaughter animals or eat meat. We shared this

food with our relatives and neighbors, who were grateful for
our help.

All of the Jews in Drohobycz suffered physical and
emotional pain. The white armbands made of cloth became
dirty and gave way to plastic ones. The plastic armbands
were sold on the streets and became very popular because
they lasted longer. I got a plastic one that didn't get dirty
and didn't have to be washed.

The armband made me feel inferior, a degraded person
who could be abused by anyone. I was marked, like an
animal.

Our Gentile friends stayed away from us. We had
known Mr. Kowalsky for many years, a retired Colonel in
the Polish army. In the autumn of 1941, my mother and I
went to see him. Mr. Kowalsky lived in a modern apartment
house with his divorced daughter. They had both frequented
my mother's chocolate store for years, and we had become
close friends.

At the entrance of the building, we removed our white
armbands so that his neighbors would not become
suspicious. We climbed the steps to the second floor and
knocked on his door. Mr. Kowalsky opened the door,
astonished to see us. His daughter wasn't home. His first
question was, "Did anyone see you enter the building?" His
face was different from the way I knew him. He was a tall
gray-haired gentleman with very bright, shining eyes, and a
friendly face. Now his eyes were cold.

Without a smile he continued, "You know, it is dangerous to enter this building."

My mother spoke quietly, "May we come in? We won't be long." My mother was dressed in a suit; she made it a point to be attractive. Kowalsky led us into the dining room, and we sat down around the large table on soft-cushioned, red velvet chairs. I noticed a beautiful Persian rug on the floor.

My mother's expression was serious and intense. She looked straight into Mr. Kowalsky's eyes. "I came to see you not for any food or money--and, by the way, we removed our armbands before we entered your building, so you don't have to worry what your neighbors will think. We came to ask you if in any way you can help Bezio escape to Hungary. We know that in Hungary the Jews are not persecuted. You must have some connections who can lead him over the border."

Mr. Kowalsky looked relieved but still anxious. His voice was soft as he wanted no one to hear us. "I have no connections with anyone," he told us, "and I'm concerned that you came here. As you know, I really don't want to get involved in any Jewish problems. Someone may have seen you coming here. Please leave."

We excused ourselves and left immediately, putting on our armbands as we got into the street. I was very disappointed by Mr. Kowalsky's behavior. I had thought of him as a friend. He used to spend hours talking with me in the store during the winters. He told me stories about hunting and nature. Now he didn't even care to talk to us. That day my mother and I also visited our maid Olga, who had worked for us for many years. She had been very close to my mother. We asked Olga if she could help hide our furs. She politely refused.

I felt abandoned by people I had considered to be my friends.

The Labor Camp

December 1941

After the disabled and sick were taken away, my family decided that I, who was approaching fourteen, should start working. To survive one had to work. The Germans were going to take away first those who were not productive.

My mother stayed home. Women over forty were in danger at work because the Germans took them away to death camps.

My sister worked at the Gartnerei, the plant nursery, along with many other young gymnasium-educated girls. But this was a dangerous place, since the Germans supervised these gardens. Once two young girls Clara's age were killed by a Gestapo man because he was not pleased with their work.

The Statishe Werkstaten was the place where my brother Jakob wanted me to work. It was at the high school, which had been converted to a factory. In the fall of 1941, realizing the need to employ skilled workers, professionals, and many young former students, Mr. Loevenberg and Mr. Hertzig approached the Gestapo. Mr. Loevenberg was a former bank executive and Mr. Hertzig a business executive. They proposed that the Germans start a factory to produce items that the Germans had a demand for. The Germans needed everything, and we could make whatever they needed with our skilled work force.

The Statishe Werkstaten had two floors and a basement. There we made toys, wheelbarrows, baskets, shoe polish, and brushes. The staff was Jewish, well trained and skilled. Some were experts in their field; others, like me, were trained on the job.

My first day on the job was in the carpentry department. An older man, a carpenter, approached me, looked me over, and said, "I see you are afraid that you wouldn't be able to handle this work. I will teach you." He had a kind face, gray hair, and dark, piercing eyes. I liked him and was grateful. He knew that I was scared. I was one of the youngest in the labor camp, and I was small and slim for carpentry work.

After several weeks I moved to the brush department, which employed about seventy-five people. Here we made brushes from scratch. We cleaned, combed, and processed horse hair for the bristles. We cut wood, drilled holes for the bristles, pushed the bristles into the holes and cut them, and then polished the brushes. Most were shoe and clothing brushes that were shipped to Germany. We also made some beautiful toys for German children, and different colors of shoe polish in wooden boxes.

We worked every day from 8 A.M. to 6 P.M. without pay and under frightening conditions. Gestapo officers like S.S. Sobota and S.S. Landau were frequent visitors. When they walked by in the factory, none of us raised our head to look at them. They carried guns and were ready to shoot anyone they disliked.

The move to the brush factory was important to me because it was less strenuous physically than carpentry. I was introduced to Mr. Bender, the factory manager. He was in his early forties and knew every phase of brush production. Mr. Bender looked at me and said, "I expect you to produce like everyone here because this is not a place to play around. Here, sit down, and I will show you how to fill these holes with bristles."

I watched his every move and rhythm and his facial expressions. His back was bent from his work, his face was pale, and he was missing a few teeth. Since my mother was baking bread, she gave me extra bread to give to Mr. Bender. She told me, "Give it to him. Maybe he will not make you work so hard and will take care of you." Every morning I brought a couple of slices of bread and put them under his table. He knew that I was the one who put it there.

I was the youngest at a large table where I sat across from men and women in their thirties. They included a lawyer, a pharmacist, a writer, and other professionals. All of us did the same work. We held a wooden handle and then pulled a wire with horse hair into a hole. We filled all the hundred or more holes, and then cut the bristles at a machine to even them out. Then the brush was finished. Eventually, I could make a brush in only fifteen minutes. I was so proficient that I became the supervisor of the entire table.

I worked in the labor camp from December 1941 until April 1943. Until October 1942 all of us workers slept at home. But after the Ghetto was created in October 1942, the basement was converted into sleeping quarters, and we were forced to sleep at the labor camp. We had communal double-tiered bunk beds. I slept on the top bed next to an elderly man who coughed continuously. The basement was not heated, and we were frozen all the time.

At seven in the morning, one of the supervisors would come in screaming at us to get up. There were a few sinks with cold water. Everyone would stand in line to wash up in a hurry.

One morning as I stood in line to wash, I noticed that the pouch that I had in my rear pants pocket was missing. My mother had made this pouch and given it to me to wear around my neck. In it, she had put one fourth of all the money we had. Jakob, Clara, mother and I each had a pouch; and each of us carried a fourth of the money from the black market grain. We were afraid that in case any one of us was taken away, all of the money would be lost, so she had divided the money into four pouches. That morning I had taken off the pouch to wash and had put it into my rear pocket.

When I saw that the pouch was missing, I became frantic. It was a fourth of everything we had! The fellow behind me --about twenty years old and a former student at the Polytechnic--watched how upset I was. He came over to me and handed me the pouch with all the money still in it. He said that he had found it on the floor. I knew that it was he who had taken it from my pocket, but even under these terrible circumstances, he had a conscience. After the war I saw him; he survived.

In the morning we were given black imitation coffee and a slice of bread. At lunch soup was served with bread or potatoes.

The camp was not guarded, but anyone found outside the camp was shot. The Gestapo knew that we couldn't escape too far. We had nowhere to go and nobody wanted to help us. We were doomed.

One morning in the fall of 1942, S.S. Sobota came into our camp to inspect. Everyone was working and very scared. Besides Mr. Loevenberg and Mr. Hertzig, there were other people working in the office. Among them was a young Jewish lawyer --I don't remember his name. He was blond, tall, and had a very pretty wife. The young lawyer accompanied S.S. Sobota, who was very tall and in his early twenties, as he inspected the facility. When they approached the stairs to the second floor, without warning Sobota stopped, took out his gun, and turned toward the young lawyer. Sobota lifted the lawyer's earlobe and shot him in the head, killing him instantly. Then he slowly walked out of the building.

I was sitting at my table pulling on the bristles when I heard one shot coming from the hallway. Right after the shot, I heard a woman scream, then silence. I looked at the two people across from me; their faces showed the same terror that I felt. What would happen next? Would we be shot now, too? A couple of people walked out into the hallway and returned immediately to their seats. They looked pale and frightened and hurried to resume their work. The tall writer at the end of my table leaned forward and whispered, "The young man who works in the office was shot. S.S. Sobota shot him, they told us, without any reason."

I kept on working, as did the others. Later some went into the hallway to see him lying dead at the bottom of the stairs. But I didn't want to see; it was too frightening for me.

The First Action

August 1942

I worked in the labor camp and I slept at home. There were rumors and reports from other cities that the Germans were rounding up Jews and taking them away. The news was frightening, but still we didn't want to believe that it could really happen.

Each day people gathered around the Judenrat to find out when the Germans and Ukrainians would start their hunt for Jews. Jews who worked for the Gestapo, like Muniek Badjan, watched and listened carefully as they worked, and passed on whatever they found out to the Judenrat.

But on a Thursday morning in August 1942, it was clear that the action was going to happen. The German and Ukrainian police were preparing for the hunt of Jews. Everyone knew, but no one could help himself.

We all were at the mercy of the Germans and Ukrainians. The Ukrainians had greeted the Germans as their liberators. Many saw an opportunity to assert themselves and hoped there was a chance to gain independence. They collaborated with the Germans in many ways.

Especially, they organized a Ukrainian police, which included some educated people. Among them was my mathematics teacher, Professor Gregoreuchuk, who became an officer in the dreaded Ukrainian police. He was a heavy-set man in his early forties. He had a very pleasant reddish face and black hair combed to the back. When he was my math teacher, he had a ready smile and was always helpful to his students. I really liked him and even trusted him with my meager savings. During the school year, I would save ten groshes (about a dime) daily. Professor Gregoreuchuk had a box in which everyone would throw their savings. He would keep track of each person's amount and at the end of the school year, we had a few zlotys to spend during our vacations.

During the German occupation, when I would approach him on the street, he ignored me.

It seemed to us that the Germans and the Ukrainians had only one objective: to get rid of the Jews. The government and the police did not spend their energy running a city government for the welfare of Drohobycz's citizens, who were also Poles and Ukrainians. Instead, they directed all their attention to destroying the Jews. The Ukrainian police were cruel, ruthless, and efficient in finding and transporting Jews--even more so than the Germans--because they knew the city well. The Nazis knew they could depend on the Ukrainian police.

In Drohobycz, Jews lived all over town. Their neighbors were Gentiles, both Polish and Ukrainian. The test came on the eve of that first hunt in August of 1942: Who would help his fellow man in need? Very few did. Panic and desperation prevailed among the Jews all over town. I saw people with bundles of meager belongings walking around with children and elderly. Everyone who knew any Gentiles approached them for help to hide. But most Gentiles turned their Jewish neighbors away. They were afraid to hide Jews, the hunted ones. In fact, when the hunt began, many Gentiles actually pointed out the Jewish homes that the Germans were looking for.

Death was approaching in town. There was nowhere to hide. We knew that we were trapped.

It couldn't be true--yet I watched it all as it was happening. The children, women, families, the elderly, entrenched in this community for a lifetime, will be torn apart? "Why?" the Rosenbergs' children asked their parents. "Why are we running to hide? Why must we go away from our houses?" How do you answer questions like that?

Most of the people in our building remained in their apartments. The shoemaker, Friedman the baker, the tailor, the barber, and others. They had no place to go to hide.

My aunts Sala and Lipcia, my mother's sisters, went to hide in their cellar. My grandfather came to our house. Those that worked in camps or factories remained at their jobs. But women, children, the elderly, and the sick remained in their homes, and the Gestapo picked them up at will.

My mother, sister, and I had no place to go. Our only hope was the coffee factory where Jakob worked. On Friday morning when we were certain that the hunt was about to begin, I decided not to go to work but to remain with the family. Clara went to work with the hope of being able to stay on the job and not to be taken away.

My brother went to the coffee factory. When Mr. Kobyla arrived, Jakob approached him. "Mr. Director," he said, "can I bring my brother and my mother here? I will hide them in the rear among the sacks of grain. You know that an action will begin this morning. I want to save their lives. Only two people."

The director looked away, his eyes buried in his work. "It's dangerous for you and me," he told Jakob. "They may come in here and find them." Jakob remained standing there, looking at Mr. Kobyla. After a minute, he turned to Jakob, "OK--only your brother."

My mother and I were waiting on the street around the corner. Jakob came to us and said that I can come in. He told our mother, "You go into the rear of the factory. I will open the door and let you in."

Inside the factory Jakob removed the last row of sacks against the wall. No one would be able to see us sitting there because of the many sacks of grain stacked in front. We sat for hours in the darkness, afraid to be discovered. It was about 11 A.M. when we heard the steps of heavy boots worn by the Ukrainian and German police. Then we heard women and children screaming. We knew the action had begun.

They dragged people from their homes all over town. They didn't spare anyone. They had it all planned to cover the entire town. With a police force of a couple hundred, the Germans systematically went through every house in town. They loaded everyone they caught into trucks, then drove them to the railroad station, where they were loaded into freight cars and shipped to the death camp Belzec in northern Poland. Later we found out about it. Most of the elderly and sick died before they reached the camp.

At the end of the warehouse, a sliver of light came through the covered window. My eyes got adjusted to the darkness, and I could see my mother in front of me. She sat, her eyes closed and tears rolling down her face. She didn't try to wipe her eyes. The tears just kept rolling down her face. She knew that her father and sisters, the only family she had, would be gone. I didn't move--only looked at her, and even at fourteen I also knew that this was the end.

I was frightened; I didn't know what to expect. I was sure that the Germans would come into the factory and drag us out into the street with the others. I was worried for my sister and the rest of the family left behind, especially my grandfather, who had remained in our home. Eventually, I fell asleep leaning against the sacks of grain.

We sat in complete silence without moving until 5 P.M., when Mr. Kobyla closed the factory. Jakob and a

Jewish co-worker, Mr. Landesman, remained.   Mr.
Landesman was the former owner of the store. They came
into the warehouse to join us for the night. Jakob was pale
and anxious; he had the responsibility for our family. He
whispered, "We are going to build a bunker under the sacks
of grain."

At about 10 P.M., when the Germans were gone from
the streets, Jakob and Mr. Landesman started working.
They removed sacks of grain all the way to the floor over a
6x4 foot area. Then they balanced planks of wood as a
"ceiling" over the area, and finally, they placed three layers
of grain sacks on top of the wood.

My mother and I sat inside. We were sheltered from
all sides by sacks of grain. We slept through the night.
Next day we heard again the Germans' marching steps and
again screams of people who had evaded the hunters the
previous day only to be caught the following day.

On the third day in the morning after the factory had
opened, two German soldiers entered the factory. We heard
their voices. They asked Mr. Kobyla, "Are there any Jews
here?"

Mr. Kobyla answered, "We have two Jews working at
the coffee roasting machine. They are the only ones who
know how to run this machine."

My brother and Mr. Landesman kept busy attending to
the machines. Then the Germans opened the door to the
warehouse where we were. They jumped up over the sacks
of grain. We heard them asking, "Is nobody hiding here?"

Mr. Kobyla answered loudly, "No."

I was scared and certain we would be found, but after jumping over many sacks near us, they left.

After they left, Mr. Kobyla sat down on his chair, very pale. Jakob came over to him and brought him cold water. Mr. Kobyla was in shock. He knew that his life was in danger in case they would have found us.

The hunt lasted for four days. During this time, we ate bread, fruits, and drank water lowered to us by my brother. Every morning Jakob moved a couple of sacks of grain and looked down on us as we lay on the floor covered with empty grain sacks. He knew that we were hungry so he cut pieces of bread and covered them with butter. He took a couple of apples, put them in a bag, and threw it to us. Then he took a pitcher of water and lowered it on a rope.

On Tuesday morning we left the factory and went home. We knew that for now the action was over because Jakob saw the Germans leave, and Jewish people were walking in the streets.

When we got home, we found our doors broken. Many items in the house were gone, but most important my grandfather was gone, and most of our neighbors in the building were not there. My sister Clara survived at her job and came home.

Next day I went to my aunts' house. I thought maybe they escaped the hunt by hiding somewhere. I found my cousins Genia and Helen and my uncle Chaim. The sisters cried uncontrollably while my uncle stood by in shock watching them.

Both of my aunts, Sala and Lipcia, were gone. Sala was frail, 47 years old. Since her marriage at the age of 18, Sala had spent all of her time attending to her family. Before the war, her husband Chaim Beck had a high position in the Galicia oil refinery. He was able to support his family well, and both of my cousins had graduated from Gymnasium. Genia, 25, had been an accountant, and Helen, 20, had attended the medical school in Lvov.

My mother's sister Lipcia was 35 years old, slim, petite, delicate, and very pretty. She had been married only two years to Chaim Lang, who died after being severely beaten by Ukrainians during the pogrom that had taken place soon after the Germans arrived in June of 1941. Before the war Lipcia ran the chocolate store with my mother, and she lived with us. Aunt Lipcia was my second mother. Since she had no children, I was very important to her. She would always give me the best chocolates in the store and never refused me anything.

My grandfather Nathan, my mother's father, was short, slim, and bearded. He lived with my Aunt Sala and always wore a black velvet yarmulka (skullcap). He was 76 years old and used to spend most of his time reading the Bible.

All three were taken away in the August 1942 action. We knew that the Germans couldn't do anything with them except kill them, but we could not say kaddish (the Jewish prayer for the dead) for them because we were not sure. How does one mourn in this situation? There were no funerals, no graves, no monuments.

My brother Szymon lived with his family in Stryj, a town about 18 kilometers from Drohobycz. Szymon was only 30 years old. He was tall and slim, with curly black hair and a narrow mustache. The last time we heard from him, he was working in a bakery. His wife, very pretty, was 31 years old and worked at home as a seamstress to supplement Szymon's income. They had a five-year-old boy named Isaac after my father and a two-year-old girl. When we found out that they had been taken away, we were all in shock and cried for many days.

It was painful for me to accept the loss of our very close family and difficult to comprehend that I would never see them again--not visit them, talk to them, or have the happy times we had had together. My brother Szymon, his wife, and children were on my mind for a long time. They had been such a beautiful family.

In our building all of the Feingold family were gone. Our neighbor Mr. Rosenberg came back from the factory to find his wife and children gone. Most women and children were gone from our building; only some working men survived.

Ours was the only entire family in the building to survive, and one of the few in town.

At my labor camp all survived because the Germans first took the workers away to the railroad station, but later released them because a German officer intervened. He wanted the factory to produce more products for the Germans for awhile. Everyone in the camp lost many family members, including Mr. Bender, our supervisor, who lost his wife and his two young children.

The next day I was back at the large table making brushes. But it wasn't the same any more. People's faces looked different. Their eyes were sad, swollen, without emotion. It seemed that no one noticed anyone sitting in front of them.

I didn't produce any brushes that day because no one had prepared any materials. Most people cried or were withdrawn. We also missed one person from the camp-- Mr. Izrael. He was about 50 years old, short, with a little beard and a smiling face. His job was to sit on a high stool and comb the raw hair by hand. When everyone returned from the railroad station, he somehow got lost and was taken away.

Mr. Bender, our supervisor, sat in the corner of the factory on a stool, motionless. I decided not to ask anyone any questions. Each of us mourned our families alone. People would leave the working area to go to the hallway and cry uncontrollably. Then they would come back and try to do some work.

The Ghetto

October 1942

After the first action our family was devastated, especially my mother. She had been very close to both of her sisters.

The families in our building were broken up. All children and most women were gone. I saw Mr. Rosenberg and Mr. Lang going to work every morning, their families gone. The apartments were empty. Old people and families no longer existed. Only about 40 percent of the Jewish population of Drohobycz survived. They were young men and women who worked, with only a few exceptions, like my mother, who had been lucky to hide and had not been discovered.

I used to sit outside in the early evening on the balcony and wait for others to come out, but nobody ever came. For several days I kept up the old habits. I waited for the girls and boys in the building to come out, meet in the yard, and talk until nighttime. But my friends were not there any more. The windows stayed dark, unlit. After a couple of evenings outside, I remained indoors.

One night in the beginning of October, Jakob and Clara

came home from work, and I came from the labor camp. As we were eating, Jakob told us, "I passed by the Judenrat and saw a notice that we have to move out of here."

We all stopped eating and stared at Jakob. How could he say such a thing so calmly, I wondered. "Where are we going to move?" I asked him.

"They say all Jews have to move to the 'Lan.'" I knew that this was the old Jewish section, where the kosher slaughterhouse, the old cemetery, and the old Great Synagogue were located.

"But how can we just leave our home?" I demanded. "We have so many nice things. Will we be able to take all those things with us?"

Jakob shrugged his shoulders and kept on eating. "I'm going tomorrow to look for a place to move," he said. "We have only two weeks to vacate this apartment."

A few days later Jakob told us that he had found an apartment in the Ghetto. It had two bedrooms and a kitchen. "I was really lucky to find this apartment with two other families," he told us. "I had to pay 500 zlotys to the people to take us in. We're going to be a total of nine people."

I could see that my mother was upset. "Where are we going to take our things--all the dishes and our furniture?" she asked.

Patiently Jakob answered, "Mom, forget all the furniture and dishes. We have room only for two beds and a table and our bedding. We will take some dishes and pots for cooking. That's it."

Within days we packed the few things, including the
two beds and a table. Jakob hired a peasant with a wagon,
who moved us to the Ghetto. We left behind most of our
belongings.

By the end of October, only about 7,000 Jews were
left in Drohobycz. All had moved into the Ghetto.

Now those who worked in labor camps slept in their
camps. My cousins Genia and Helen remained at the
Herawka camp, and I slept in the basement of the Statishe
Werkstaten. Clara and Jakob, who had permits to work
outside the Ghetto, slept in the apartment. My mother, who
wasn't working, stayed all the time in the Ghetto.

The broken walls and doors in the Ghetto were a
reminder of the frequent assaults by the German and
Ukrainian police. Dirt and foul smells filled the streets.
Even the Great Synagogue was ruined. Inside, the ark was
gone, and so were the benches that I used to sit on when I
attended services with my father.

The Ghetto streets were usually empty during the day
since most who survived were at work and others were
staying indoors. The Ghetto had no walls or gates because
Jews knew where they were supposed to live and move
about, and Germans knew that Jews couldn't go far without
being caught.

I visited the Ghetto frequently after work because I had
a need to be in touch with my family. Usually I would
remove my white armband, jump over the back fence, and
walk to my family's new home. I felt safer with my family,

and they also wanted to see me frequently even though there was the risk that I might be caught and shot.

The apartment in the Ghetto had bare walls. In the kitchen were a sink with cold running water, a gas stove, and a closet. The closet was a surprise because apartments in Drohobycz had no wall closets. Clothes and other things were kept in cupboards or in movable wooden closets. I noticed the closet immediately and hurried to tell Jakob about it. The closet was about three feet wide and three feet deep. We realized that it could be camouflaged and would make a good hiding place.

We hired a carpenter, who made a wooden board with many pegs that exactly fit the closet. On this rack we hung our clothing--dresses, shirts, pants, blouses, and skirts. The rack could be pushed away so that my mother could enter the closet to hide. After she was inside, we pushed the rack back flat as far as it would go. It made a false back to the closet, and no one could tell that she was hidden behind it.

This closet gave us some security in situations when the Germans would come suddenly to the Ghetto to take away people. But it served a special need for my mother.

Each day before Jakob left for work, he put mother into the closet for the whole day. And every evening when he came home, he let her out for the night. This routine went on from early October through March. My mother sat in the closet through the endless days, listening to the goings-on around her. Frequently the hunters entered the building, broke down doors, and ransacked apartments looking for Jews.

One day my mother heard the cry of a young woman in the apartment above us. She and her one-year-old baby were being dragged down the stairs into the courtyard. Then she heard two shots, and all was quiet. They were killed by a German Gestapo man. My mother had known the woman well. She was young and beautiful, the wife of a prominent lawyer.

Sitting in her dark closet, my mother listened to the street below. Another day she heard a young boy sobbing as he ran after his father. "Don't take my father!" he cried. "Don't take away my father!"

At times when she felt the Germans wouldn't enter the Ghetto, she stayed outside the closet. One day she looked out the window and saw Germans approaching the building with a truck full of clothing and other personal things. They weren't hunting for people that day. Since they planned to liquidate the Ghetto, they were removing all personal items beforehand. My mother put on her best winter coat so they wouldn't take it away with the other items in the room. She took other things she valued and put them into her bed, covering everything with a bedspread. When the Germans came into the apartment, they opened her bed, took everything away, and ripped the lining out of her coat, looking for valuables. They left her wearing her coat.

The wall at Kowalska Street where hundreds
of Jews were executed.

The Second Action

November 1942

Again the inevitable was coming. In mid-November when all the Jews were in the Ghetto, the Germans decided it was time for the second hunt of Jews. The second action started on November 19, 1942, which was called "Bloody Thursday."

The night before I had stayed in the Ghetto because rumors were that the second action would start the next day. We got up early. My brother Jakob didn't ask his Ukrainian boss to hide us this time because it was obvious that after a close call in the first action, Mr. Kobyla would not favor our repeat visit to the coffee roasting factory.

Jakob had another plan. He knew that my mother would not be safe in the Ghetto, and he also didn't trust the Statishe Werkstaten for me to be at the mercy of the hunters. Therefore, without Mr. Kobyla's knowledge, he got keys from the coffee factory's warehouse on the other side of town and took us there. We took with us two members of Mr. Landesman's family, Jakob's co-worker. Jakob gave us bread, water, and fruits, and locked us in with large padlocks to discourage the Germans from breaking them.

My sister Clara decided to go to her job, where she felt safe because she had survived the first action there.

Meanwhile, the entire German and Ukrainian police force decided to get drunk before they entered the Ghetto and also moved around all over town. The Gestapo, among them S.S. Gunter, became especially vicious. They were killing every Jew they found on the streets. Among those killed that day was Bruno Shulz, the world-famous writer and artist, who was killed by S.S. Gunter.

About 11 in the morning, as Jakob was returning from where he had hidden us, the action began. Near Jakob's coffee factory S.S. Landau was standing with his revolver in his hand. Landau shouted at Jakob, "You dirty, disgusting Jew!" and turned his gun on Jakob. Scared for his life, Jakob begged him not to shoot, pointing to the coffee factory where he was going. S.S. Landau looked at Jakob. "Go ahead fast," he ordered. "You are lucky that I like coffee."

The second action lasted seven days. This time, the Germans wanted to make sure they got most Jews. They killed scores on the streets, especially against the wall on Kowalska Street across from the coffee factory, where Jakob stayed all through the seven-day action. My brother watched in panic as Gestapo men grabbed Jews, going and coming from work, pushed them against the wall, and shot them. Jakob saw a man he knew, a carpenter. The hunter asked him to put down his tools and then shot him in the head against the wall.

In the warehouse where Jakob had hidden us, we found a back room where we stayed during the day. The room had no windows, and boxes of coffee were stored there. All four of us sat on the bench, and at night we slept in the corner of the warehouse on the floor.

During the seven-day action, the Gentiles were not on the streets; they stayed indoors. We heard only German S.S. men and Ukrainian policemen walking by. They would try to open the warehouse doors but were discouraged by the huge padlocks. Also, the fact that the warehouse was far from the Ghetto made our hiding place safer. The Germans put those unfortunates they had rounded up onto trucks and drove them immediately to Bronica Ravine. There they were shot and buried in mass graves.

On the seventh day my sister Clara, who was terribly anxious about our fate, came by the warehouse. She knocked at the window, looking for us. When we saw Clara, we knew that the action was over. The German and Ukrainian police were off the streets. Gentiles were walking around, and life had become more normal again.

A while later Jakob came and opened the doors, and we returned to our apartment in the Ghetto. We found our apartment ransacked, the front door broken, and my uncle Chaim gone. Chaim had remained in our Ghetto apartment hidden in the closet. But since he suffered from asthma, he couldn't be without air and had left the closet. The hunters returned repeatedly to the Ghetto each day, and they found Uncle Chaim and took him away.

After that, when we walked through the Ghetto, it was obvious that most of the Jews had been taken away. Only a couple of thousand Jews remained alive.

My Sister Clara

Early December, 1942

We became desperate; there was no place to hide. We felt lucky to have survived until now, but we knew that we were doomed. Soon there would be another action, and any day the Ghetto could be liquidated.

My sister Clara was 26 years old. She had black hair, black eyes, pretty features, red cheeks, and a smooth skin. Clara was vibrant and full of life. She wanted to live. She planned for marriage and children.

Clara worked at the Gartnerei, the plant nursery, and slept at home. At work she noticed that a number of people left the camp--most likely for hiding places. Clara worked with a man about 30 whom she had known for a year, and she cared for him. He was tall and handsome, a butcher by trade, with a very kind face. I thought of them as the perfect couple. Clara and her boyfriend often talked about going away with other people to hide in the forest.

One day after work Clara approached my mother. Clara had been only ten when my mother married my father, so my mother had really raised her. Clara was very close to my mother, respected her, and loved her. She knew that my mother would understand her.

That afternoon, as she sat and talked with my mother, Clara's face was pale, anxious, intense. I understood that she had something very important to say to my mother.

When I came closer, I heard Clara saying, "I trust these people, Mom. There are about ten of us. They built a bunker in the forest, and they are willing to take me along. My boyfriend is going, and I want to go there, too."

Clara's face was full of pain. "I am young, Mom. I want to live, to be married and have children. We are going to die here." She raised her voice, "The Ghetto will be liquidated soon. Can't you see?" Clara really wasn't asking; she was telling my mother that she was going.

My mother's face showed her confusion. "Let's stay together, Clara, darling. What will happen to all of us will happen to you. These people are strangers; you need to be with us."

"I must go," Clara insisted. "I can't take it any more."

My mother looked puzzled. "I don't really know what we are going to do. Maybe you are right. Maybe you will survive in the forest."

I understood Clara. She had an opportunity that we didn't have at that time. We were confined to the Ghetto and camp and had no place to hide. Clara felt she had a chance; she wanted to live and be with her boyfriend.

Clara was sitting on the bed with my mother, and Jakob and I sat next to her. Jakob asked her about the bunker in the forest, but she really didn't know much about

it. She relied on the others who were already there, and she
trusted them.

That evening was the last time I saw Clara. I had to
return to the labor camp that night. My mother told me that
when Clara left next morning for work, she took with her a
few personal belongings. After work Clara and her
boyfriend went to the forest.

We didn't hear from Clara and really didn't expect to
because she was deep in the forest, unable to communicate
with us. In a way we were happy for her. All of us hoped
that she had found a way to survive because we had no place
to hide for a long period. One early evening at the end of
January, a man whom Jakob knew came rushing into our
apartment. "Jakob," he cried, "I just saw your sister on a
truck screaming to me as I walked on Samborska Street.
`Get Jakob Mayer!' she was screaming. `The Germans are
taking us away!'"

We knew that the Germans were taking Jews they
found in the forest and anywhere outside the Ghetto to
Bronica Ravine five kilometers from the city. The truck that
Clara was on was headed in the direction of Bronica.

Jakob ran immediately to see people to try to find her
in jail. "If they've taken her to jail," he told us, "I know a
lot of people in the Judenrat and some Germans. I may be
able to save her-- if only I can find her in jail."

But Clara never had a chance. Jakob was told that the
Germans had discovered the bunker in the forest and had

taken Clara and the others directly to Bronica to be shot at the ravine.

We were devastated by the loss of Clara. She had gambled and lost. But she had the right idea because at that time it was better to be in the forest than to stay in the Ghetto.

Desperation

December 1942

The Ghetto was doomed. As I worked in the camp, I worried about my mother and brother who still lived there. Many Jews had already left the Ghetto--to hide somewhere, to work in labor camps, or to run into the forest to escape the final hunt.

On one of my trips to the Ghetto, Jakob told me about a possible hiding place. For a sum of money, a Gentile who owned a house near the labor camp would allow our family to hide in the cellar. I decided to check out the Gentile owner and the hiding place.

The next day after work I went to his house. When he opened the door cautiously, I told him who I was and what I'd come for. He took me into the back room, opened a trap door, and motioned me down the steps. "There are three people already here," he told me.

As I walked down the few steps, darkness engulfed me. A little dim light came from a small window just above the ground. The owner had piled stones outside against the window to conceal it.

I walked down into darkness and the smell of damp earth. I could see three people lying in the middle of this cellar. It was really a crawl space less than three feet high.

No one could sit up or walk. The ground was damp and cold. The owner closed the trap door behind me, and I felt trapped and panicky. I lay there in my coat on the freezing ground. In the corner was a pot for toilet use. There were a few slices of bread and a pot of water on a cloth on the ground.

My mind churned. It is impossible to live here, I thought. I must get out of here. We will not be able to survive here long. No, it is impossible, I thought. I felt sorry for the three people who lay at one end of the cellar. They looked exhausted and ill. I wondered how long they would last in such terrible conditions.

I had to wait until morning for the owner to open the cellar for me to get out. I felt enormously relieved to be out of there, to walk upright, to see daylight and breathe fresh air. I hurried back to the camp.

That night I told Jakob that this place was not for us, that we could not possibly survive there. The question again was, where do we hide before we are taken away?

A week later Jakob arrived unexpectedly in camp on a dark night. "Bezio, I have come to talk to you." I could see that he was frightened. He had come without his white armband and had to jump over the fence to get into the camp. He found me in my work area, where I sat talking with the other workers before we went to sleep in the cramped quarters in the basement. Everyone was surprised to see Jakob since he was not working there.

Jakob took me to the back of the room so we could talk privately. "I was at the Judenrat today," he paused and took a deep breath, "and the talk is that it's the end. The Ghetto will be liquidated sometime in the next few days. After that, this camp will go also." Jakob looked straight at me with his steady blue eyes.

"Listen carefully, Bezio. We must stick together." His voice was strong. "Mr. Rubin, who is working in the German barracks, takes care of the horse stables. I met him yesterday in the Ghetto. He told me that he can hide us. You know this is the end, and we have absolutely no place to go. When they liquidate the Ghetto, they will take everyone away and destroy our homes."

"But, Jakob, how are we going to live in the barracks? There are Germans all over the place there."

Jakob nodded, "Mr. Rubin told me that there is an attic over the stables, and we will be able to stay there. He will deliver food for us. I talked to Mom about this already. We will leave the day after tomorrow very early in the morning. That way we'll get to the barracks before the soldiers are awake. He gave me all the instructions. Tomorrow night, you make sure to leave the camp and come to our apartment. You'll sleep there overnight so we can leave together to go to the German barracks."

Jakob sounded confident, and I knew that he must be right about this plan. He wanted the best for all of us--to save us.

The next night when I came to the Ghetto, I found my mother preparing three knapsacks--one for each of us. Jakob had arranged to meet Mr. Rubin at the rear of the barracks before 6 A.M., and the barracks were several kilometers outside of town.

It was still very dark when we woke. We put on our coats and galoshes and quickly left the Ghetto. Soon we were walking across the fields so we would not be noticed on the streets. In the starlight, the fields were covered with snow as far as I could see. Behind us the rooftops of Drohobycz were all white; some houses had lights in their windows.

It was freezing cold, and an icy wind blew in my face. In some places the snow was so deep that I sank into it above my knees. Walking through the deep snow was very difficult, especially for my mother.

All of a sudden I noticed that the galosh was missing from my right foot. I wanted to go back to look for it, but Jakob stopped me. "No, Bezio, we can't stop. We must go on." It upset me because my foot was wet and numb with cold.

We walked--or pushed our way through the snow--for more than an hour. Before the sun rose, we reached the fenced-in barracks. Just as we approached the barracks, we heard Mr. Rubin's voice from behind the fence. "You are late!" he scolded, and then he softened his voice when he saw how exhausted we were. "But it's still OK. Jump over and run right into this stable where I left the door open."

Jakob and I pushed my mother over the fence, and then we both jumped over. We scurried into the stable, desperately afraid a German soldier would see us. I was scared to be among all the horses, snorting and stamping in their stalls. The smell of the stable was overpowering--a mixture of horse manure and sweet-smelling straw.

Quickly we climbed the tall ladder that led to the attic. I felt relieved to be in the attic at last. I immediately removed my wet shoes. My mother helped me take off my coat and covered me with a small blanket she had carried in her knapsack.

I looked around. Six other people lay on the straw spread across the floor. I recognized a young Orthodox couple. He was one of the few Jews in Drohobycz who still kept his beard and wore a skullcap. Even the head rabbi had shaved his beard so that he wouldn't be taunted by Poles and Ukrainians. The bearded young man whispered close to my ear, "You have to be completely quiet because German soldiers are all over this yard. Any noise will doom us immediately." I wondered how long he and the others had been there.

My mother was exhausted from her ordeal. Jakob and I had helped her through the deep snow, but she was not strong. She lay down and fell asleep immediately. I watched her sleeping on the straw and thought, how odd it is to be here.

The young man whispered to me and pointed, "You see, there is bread and water in this corner, and on the other

side we have a pail that we use for a toilet. Mr. Rubin picks
it up every morning."

Here we could sit up, at least, but the ceiling was too
low for anyone to stand. Daylight filtered through cracks in
the wooden walls. The attic was freezing cold.

After a while, Jakob spoke softly to me, "This is not a
place to be for long. Sooner or later they will discover us
when Mr. Rubin may be taken away from his job."

"But Jakob," I whispered, "what else can we do? We
have nowhere else to go. Maybe a miracle will happen and
the Russians will come soon." I was trying to cheer myself
up as well as Jakob. He only looked at me without saying
anything more.

Three days and nights passed. We lay down or sat all
the time without talking. Our only contact with the outside
was Mr. Rubin. Every day he would venture to the Ghetto
and to the Judenrat to hear any rumors about the fate of the
Jews left in the Ghetto. On the fourth evening Mr. Rubin
announced, "The liquidation of the Ghetto will not take place
now--not yet. That's what they told me at the Judenrat."

Silently--but with great joy and relief--I hugged my
mother and Jakob. "Now we must return unnoticed to the
Ghetto," Jakob whispered hoarsely. "We need to wait for
tomorrow early morning and again jump the fence and walk
through the fields while it is still dark. We will not wear our
armbands until we reach the Ghetto."

So we rose again in darkness and struggled across the snow-covered fields to the Ghetto.

"It was the craziest thing to do what we did," Jakob told me as we walked in the deep snow. "We were right there in the lion's den!"

"Thank God," I said, "that I only lost one galosh."

The Connection

January 1943

At times my mother ventured out to shop for groceries. There was one small grocery store in the Ghetto run by Mr. Kupferberg. He took a chance to keep it open during the days when the German police were not in the Ghetto. He lived above the store, bribing some officers to tell him when it was safe to keep his store open. Mr. Kupferberg's store was also a meeting place, where we could find out about the happenings in our Ghetto and in the world.

One cold morning Jakob anticipated a quiet day. He decided to let mother stay out of the closet so she would be able to buy groceries at Mr. Kupferberg's store and prepare a meal. About noon mother dressed warmly. Before she left the apartment, she looked into the streets through the half- frozen window to make sure there were people walking around and no Germans on the street.

As my mother was waiting for Mr. Kupferberg to weigh her flour, Mrs. Schwartz walked in. Mrs. Schwartz was a medium height woman, about 43, with a dark complexion, curly black hair, and black piercing eyes. She had a high-pitched voice and always talked with forceful intensity until her breath ran out.

The Schwartz family consisted of mother, father, two daughters--Recia, 21, and Lotka, 19--and a son Alus, 15, who was my age. Before the Germans forced all Jews into the Ghetto, the Schwartz family lived in a one-story house they owned at 59 Boryslawska Street. The house had four rooms, a basement, and an attic for storage. Behind the house was a big lot with a dry well. The Schwartzes had stopped using the well when water lines on the street made water available at an automatic pump on every block.

Near their home the Schwartzes owned a candle factory. Mr. Schwartz and a few workers manufactured candles and shipped them all over Poland. Mr. Schwartz was a short, thin, dark-skinned man, who spoke very softly. When his wife spoke, he kept quiet. Mrs. Schwartz had control over the entire family, and she made the decisions, especially when it came to important matters.

Mrs. Schwartz knew my mother casually from before the war, so she approached her in the grocery store. They talked for awhile. Mrs. Schwartz knew that she could confide to my mother her most important secret--about the hiding place of her family.

Mrs. Schwartz asked my mother to go outside with her. When she was sure no one could overhear, she asked my mother the most important question: "Do you have any money?"

"Yes," my mother answered, "I have some."

Mrs. Schwartz continued. "Then I can talk to you because we can build a bunker in my house where a

Ukrainian lives now. As you see, Mrs. Mayer," Mrs. Schwartz pointed to the street, "this is the end. The Germans and the Ukrainians will come soon to take all of us away--the few of us who remain after the two actions. I have to tell you everything from the beginning," she continued.

"All through the years we had Mr. Kaczmarek working for us. He is a decent Ukrainian with a family, and we treated him well. When the Germans came, Mr. Kaczmarek became manager of the candle factory. Eventually he hid our family in the factory during and after the actions. When we moved into the Ghetto and our house was empty, Mr. Kaczmarek told Ivan Bur to move in there. Ivan is a young Ukrainian who works in the candle factory, and since he lives in a village nearby, it would be much closer for him to get to work.

"A couple of weeks ago," Mrs. Schwartz lowered her voice to a whisper, "Mr. Kaczmarek talked to Ivan and asked him if he would like to hide Jews for money. Ivan said, `OK, for a price I will do it.'

"Then Kaczmarek said, `A bunker will be built under this house, and you will live here and buy food for these people.' Ivan agreed."

Mrs. Schwartz paused to take a breath. "Here we are, Mrs. Mayer. Now we need someone to organize the labor and pay for building the bunker and also to pay Ivan twenty golden dollars for each of us because I have no money. And since I am the person who found Ivan and the place to build the bunker, the others including you will have to pay the money for my family as well as for themselves."

My mother knew that Mr. Schwartz was a quiet man who didn't know many people in town and wasn't the type to organize the building of a bunker. Someone would have to find a person to build the bunker and materials would have to be purchased. She realized immediately that Jakob was the perfect person to put it all together. Few people would be able to accomplish such a task under these circumstances.

So my mother immediately accepted Mrs. Schwartz's offer. She told Mrs. Schwartz to bring Ivan to our apartment to talk over the deal.

That evening I came home to visit my mother and Jakob. My mother told us enthusiastically about the most wonderful meeting she had in Mr. Kupferberg's store. "Imagine," she said, "I seldom go out and here I meet Mrs. Schwartz, who knows a Gentile man who will hide us. It's a miracle."

She kept on repeating the word "miracle." She told us the details of her entire conversation with Mrs. Schwartz. "She says we will have double protection. She has full confidence in Mr. Kaczmarek, who will guide young Mr. Ivan Bur on how to proceed with hiding Jews. And at the same time Ivan will think twice before taking away our money and abandoning us, because Kaczmarek knows about the deal."

I was feeling something I hadn't felt in years--a small, growing glow of hope. My voice was ecstatic. "Jakob, I can't believe it's true. At last we have the chance we've been waiting for. Let's give him all the money and save ourselves. This is our only opportunity to save our lives. We don't know what can happen, but here is some chance."

Jakob, his head bowed, looked puzzled. He hadn't expected anything like this to happen. "Let's meet this Ivan and see who he is," he said, "and, most important, if we can trust him." Then he looked at my mother's glowing face. "Mom, it's wonderful that you met Mrs. Schwartz today. It is a miracle." He paused. "But it all sounds too good to be true. The Russians are 2,000 kilometers from here. Who knows how long it will take to liberate us. We need to build a bunker for a long term."

My mother came over to Jakob. "Jakob," she said, "take these diamonds and exchange them for dollars." My mother held out in her open palm two diamonds that she'd had for years. She'd been hiding them inside raw potatoes in a bag in the kitchen. "We will give everything to Ivan if he hides us. I trust Mrs. Schwartz. She tells us the truth. Let's go on with it."

Ivan Bur in 1943, during the time
he was hiding us.

Meeting Ivan

The next evening

I was very anxious and excited. Again I needed to go back to the Ghetto because Mrs. Schwartz was bringing Ivan to meet my mother and Jakob. It was a Saturday night.

The backyard of my labor camp was deserted. At about 8 P.M., I put on my coat, scarf, and hat, and walked quickly across the yard. All workers at the camp were resting at the working area, about to proceed to their sleeping quarters in the basement. It was dark, and I had no problem jumping over the tall fence.

I removed my white armband and walked toward the street. I put up my coat collar, put my hands into my pockets, and walked toward the Ghetto. Looking in all directions, I realized that no one was on the street. Gentiles usually didn't walk after dark, so it was dangerous to be seen on the streets. This time I decided to go through the center of the Rynek, the town square, with its high tower overlooking the city. The trees and rooftops were covered with snow sparkling in the dark. I thought, how lucky are these people in homes, who can live in peace and not be threatened with death. They have no fear for their lives, I thought. Their children are safe, and the families are together. Tomorrow they will put on their good clothing and go to church.

My pace quickened as I approached the town square. I made a point to look only in front of me and move forward, so I would not look nervous or suspicious. As I crossed the center of the square, two German police walked out of an alley. My heart beat faster, but I kept on walking at my regular pace. The Germans walked toward me, glanced at me, and continued to talk and laugh to each other as they passed me. I continued toward the Ghetto, now at a much faster pace and with great anticipation.

As I entered the house, I ran up the stairs, opened the door, and found Mrs. Schwartz and a young man standing in the middle of the room, talking with my mother and Jakob. (The people who shared the apartment stayed in their own room and were not involved in this plan.) I knew that the man was Ivan Bur. Mrs. Schwartz had a job to convince Jakob that Ivan could be trusted, and to talk Ivan into having the bunker built under his house for more money than he had ever seen before.

When I looked at Ivan, he gave me the impression that he couldn't be trusted. He was very young, in his early twenties, with a cavalier posture and a smirky expression. He was tall, slim, blue-eyed, with blond hair and a narrow mustache. With his leather half coat and polished boots, he looked like a typical young Ukrainian nationalist. These Ukrainians were fighting for the independence of the

Ukraine and were collaborators of the Germans. They
certainly didn't care about the welfare of the Jews.

But after talking awhile, I realized that I could be
mistaken about Ivan's character and his intentions. I saw
him as an adventurous, self-assured young man, who was
challenging the Nazis and at the same time making a fortune.
He was willing to take risks. In my eyes he was a very
complex character. He didn't act as if he loved Jews or
hated them. It was never clear to me what his real motives
were for taking on a risky task like this.

Jakob reminded him, "You know, Ivan, it will take a
lot of work. You must be strong. You have to be with us
all the time during the building of the bunker and afterward
during our stay."

Smiling, Ivan reassured him, "You will see that I can
work well with you." He looked unafraid and very
confident.

Mrs. Schwartz kept on interjecting in Yiddish,
"Kaczmarek is watching him. Therefore, Ivan will not turn
on us. He will be afraid to surrender us to the Nazis."

Ivan looked at Mrs. Schwartz and laughed. "I know
what you are saying. I will take care of things, don't
worry."

Jakob realized that this was an opportunity that he
could not miss. "We have a deal," he told Ivan. "I will give
you eight golden twenty dollar pieces for all of us. Now we
are going to find others who have money." We needed
money for materials and to pay the builder, and enough

money for food during what we expected would be a long stay in the bunker--until the Russians reach Drohobycz. After Stalingrad we knew that the Red Army will be back. It was just a question of when.

Ivan was not reluctant but anxious to go on with the project. He saw an opportunity not only to become rich, but also to feel important. He knew that Jewish lives depended on him, and he liked that.

Our meeting with Ivan lasted about half an hour. He was standing the whole time, conscious of the fact that he was in the Ghetto. At the end of the meeting, Jakob told Ivan that he would find someone who knows how to build a bunker, bring him over to the house, and have him make a plan.

Ivan put on his hat and said, "Come over tomorrow night. We will plan the bunker." He seemed totally at ease. His voice was optimistic and without fear.

Mrs. Schwartz stayed on talking to Jakob, again reassuring him about Ivan.

Instead of returning to the camp, I remained home for the night because of the excitement. All of a sudden we saw some hope, a way out of this terrible situation that was about to consume us.

Jakob said to me, "I think there may be a man in the Ghetto who can build the bunker. His name is Aron Shapiro. He is an excellent carpenter, and I hear that he builds bunkers. I've known him since childhood. Tomorrow morning I'll look for him and we'll take him to Ivan's house."

"Jakob," I said, "I'm going to be here tomorrow night. I must go with you." I had just turned fifteen, but I had a need to be involved in building the bunker. I participated in every move.

Aron, the Genius

January 1943

All that night and the next day the bunker was on my mind. I couldn't wait to see Ivan's house and meet Aron Shapiro and have the bunker started. I returned to camp early next morning. Right after work I took off my armband and hurried to the Ghetto. My mother and I waited about an hour until Jakob and Aron arrived.

Aron was short and muscular with large arms. He had a square face, black hair, and black burning eyes. He was about 30 years old, an observant Jew, married, with a two-year-old son.

Aron and his four brothers had built a bunker for their large extended family of about 80 people. Aron and his family lived there now. This bunker was ingeniously built under an apartment building in the Ghetto. The bunker was self-contained, Aron told us. It had running water, even a shower, and was stocked with food for one year. There was an escape exit to the city's sewer system.

Jakob, Aron, and I removed our armbands and proceeded out of the Ghetto toward Ivan's house. We were to meet Ivan at 59 Boryslawska Street, about three kilometers from the Ghetto.

Jakob walked with Aron. I followed a block behind so that we would not be suspicious as a group. There was heavy snow on the ground, and we walked rapidly through the dark, frozen streets. All of a sudden we saw two policemen walking toward us. Jakob and Aron turned into the first house entrance they came to, and I turned down another street. A half hour later we met at Ivan's house, scared and tired.

The house was small, about 30 by 30 feet, built of bricks. It had four rooms on one level and an attic. Steps led down to a cellar under the rear of the house. Because the lot slanted steeply away from the street, there was no basement under the front of the house. The house had a front porch and a large backyard, with scattered trees and an old dry well in the rear. On the left, facing the street, the neighbor's house was quite close. On the right was an empty area and then another neighbor, not so close.

The house had electricity and gas but no running water. People got water from pumps on each block, and every day people would pump water into pails and carry them into their homes. There was a sewer line from Ivan's house that led into the field in the rear of the house. The outhouse was also in the backyard.

Immediately we went down to the cellar. It was about half the size of the house--15 feet wide and 30 feet long-- and had a cement floor. When we came into the cellar, we noticed a brick wall on the side facing the street. Ivan brought a couple of blankets for Jakob and me to sit on while Aron walked around the house. Aron examined the utilities, then the backyard. He noticed things that other people didn't. He was ingenious and never ran out of ideas. He was a plumber, carpenter, electrician--a true jack-of-all trades. But most important, he was courageous and brilliant.

It took Aron about one hour to examine the entire house including the location of the sewer. By this time it was about 10 P.M. Aron came back into the cellar and sat down with us on a blanket. We could tell from looking at him that he was feeling optimistic. "You see the brick wall in front of you? We will build the bunker behind this wall-- under the front part of the house. It's a big job, but it can be done. You have electricity here and gas for cooking, but you have no water. We have to think how to have water."

Jakob asked, "Where are we going to get water? Ivan can't carry water for all these people."

"My next question," Aron said calmly, "is how many people will you have here?"

"We need room for sixteen people. We will be hiding here until the Russian army liberates Drohobycz," Jakob answered.

"Well," Aron was thoughtful. "We can do it, and I think we can have water and a sewer here, too."

Aron took a hammer and knocked out a few bricks from the wall, exposing the earth beneath the front part of the house. I watched Jakob. He had been at first hopeful about the job, but now he looked uncertain. Jakob turned to Aron, "I don't know how this will work out. How can we dig out so much dirt? Where are we going to get the materials? Do you think it's a good idea, Aron?" Aron didn't answer right away.

Jakob walked over to Aron and asked again, "Is it really possible to build a bunker here, and be safe, with the neighbors around us? Living underground?"

Aron looked straight in Jakob's eyes. "Do you think you have a choice? I can build it, but I don't guarantee that you will survive."

Of all of us, Ivan was the most confident. He was young, naive, and without fear. "Jakob," he kept saying, "can't you see Aron knows how to do it? Aron is smart--a genius."

Jakob looked tired and sad. His eyes were red from the stale cellar air. He turned to me, "We will go on, Bezio. We have no choice."

A few minutes later I left Ivan's house and returned to the Ghetto to tell my mother what Aron had said. She was waiting impatiently to hear from us. Jakob and Aron remained in Ivan's house overnight.

The Building Plan

Next evening, January 1943

After work the next day I hurried to the Ghetto. I wanted to know what had happened. What kind of plan did Aron have? How will he start? So much earth to remove and where can it go? Where will we eat, sleep, and use the bathroom? My mind was full of questions. When I arrived, I found Jakob, Aron, and my mother sitting at the table in our room. Aron had a brown paper on the table with a plan that he had drawn in pencil.

Aron was looking at Jakob and gesturing with his large, powerful hands, emphasizing how he will remove the earth from under the front of the house and get rid of it in the dry well. "You see, Jakob, the well in the back of the house is very deep. We will dispose of most of the earth there. We need people to dig it out and carry it at night and dump it in the well."

"We have five people to work with you," Jakob told him, "Mr. Schwartz; his son Alus; Manek Bergwerk, his nephew; Hersh Ekstein; and myself."

"We will dump most of the earth down the well," Aron continued, "but we will save enough earth in the cellar to fill all around the bunker. We will build the bunker all out of wood--ceiling, walls, and floor--five feet below the house floor, five feet below the cellar floor, and five feet behind the brick wall. And when the bunker is finished, we will fill in these five-foot spaces entirely with the earth we have saved. That way if any Germans or Ukrainians break through the house floor or the cellar wall looking for Jews, they will find only earth."

I was standing behind Jakob, looking down on Aron's plan. All of a sudden a thought came to me. "How are we going to *breathe*?"

"You see, Bezio," Aron showed us on the plan, "the air will come from the sewer into the toilet and then into the bunker. And we will extend the house's chimney down into the bunker so air will come out of it, too. Here I will build a stove with an oven in the rear, a toilet will be connected to the sewer here, and all along the side a six-foot-wide row of wooden planks, where you will sit and sleep on."

"But, Aron," I asked, "what about water?"

Aron got up from the table and gestured to me. "You think I forgot about water? You will have two cisterns, holes in the ground," he showed me two fingers and continued in a Chasidic-type chanting voice. "You will have plenty of water when it rains, or too much water when it rains a lot, or no water if it doesn't rain."

Aron turned to Jakob, "Here is a list of materials that I must have to do the job. We must have them soon, after we finish digging," and he said goodbye and left.

Jakob looked at the list in his hand. Aron wanted different sizes of hard wood for the bunker and also wood for building a fence around Ivan's house. This was a ploy to divert the neighbors' attention because wood was going to be delivered and the sounds of building would be heard. When we started building the bunker, Ivan was going to start building a fence. And he would also repair his front porch, which would explain the delivery of the wood, cement, pipes, and electrical wiring that were also on Aron's list.

Jakob looked more cheerful. "I know Mr. Holtzman, who works in the lumber yard outside the Ghetto," he told me. "I'm going to his house right now to talk with him. I will pay him well. Maybe we can get the supplies through him."

Mr. Holtzman's family had owned the lumber yard before the war. He knew the business well, and the new Gentile owners needed him, so they let him work there.

Holtzman lived in the Ghetto a short distance from us. An hour later Jakob was back. I noticed he was excited after talking to Holtzman. "Bezio," he told me, "we worked out a plan that I'm going to pay him for everything, and then he will bribe the Gentile workers in the yard to keep them quiet. He will prepare the items on Aron's list for Ivan to pick up." Jakob's blue eyes shone, "We are going to make it!"

Jakob hadn't explained to Holtzman why he needed the lumber or why a Gentile man would pick it up. In those days there was a shortage of lumber but for money you got everything, and all kinds of business deals took place.

A few days later Ivan borrowed a horse and buggy from a farmer in the village, went to the lumber yard, and brought back all the lumber and other supplies. He deposited everything in the cellar.

Later that week Ivan started working on a fence around the house. Building a fence in February was very unsual. Therefore, Ivan erected only a partial frame to demonstrate to the neighbors the reason for the delivery of lumber.

Secrecy had to prevail, especially from the neighbors. Gentiles were quick to interpret any suspicious acts or movements as an indication that Jews were hiding. Everyone was on guard during this time. Ivan's undertaking in the midst of a Gentile neighborhood was truly a daring act.

The house where the underground bunker was built and where forty-five Jews lived up to eighteen months and survived the Holocaust.

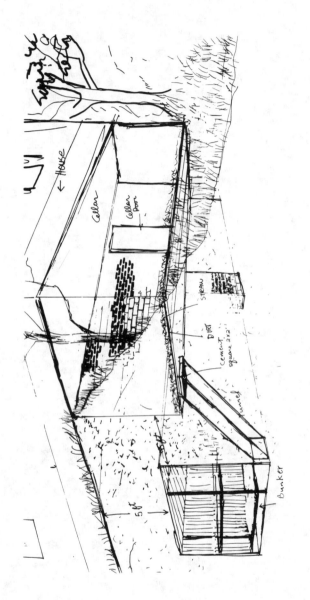

The cellar and the bunker as it looked underground.

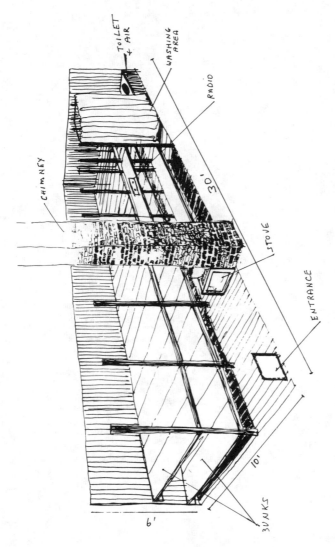

INSIDE OF THE BUNKER--upper and lower bunks for forty-five people. It also contained a toilet, radio, and stove. Air was coming from the sewer through the toilet.

Labels on drawing: TOILET + AIR, WASHING AREA, RADIO, CHIMNEY, STOVE, ENTRANCE, BUNKS, 30', 10', 6'

Building the Bunker

End of January 1943

About ten days after we first met Ivan, Jakob told Mr. Kobyla, the manager of the coffee factory, that he would not be working any more. "I am leaving to hide. There are only a handful of Jews in the Ghetto, and we know that it will be liquidated soon. My mother and brother are the only ones left from our entire family."

Mr. Kobyla looked at Jakob sadly. He put his hand into his pocket, took a handful of zlotys, and handed them to him. "Jakob, I wish I could do more for you. Take it, and I wish you the best of luck." Jakob thanked him, realizing that if not for Mr. Kobyla, he wouldn't have money to build the bunker.

That night Jakob put mother into the closet. He attached a rope to the inside of the rack so that she could enter the closet and pull on the rope to close the rack behind her. Mother tried it out several times. By midnight she had perfected it, and Jakob knew that he could leave her in the Ghetto while he went to live in Ivan's house to help build the bunker. Mother would have to attend to herself until she would be able to leave the Ghetto permanently-- after the bunker was finished.

The next night I went to Ivan's house. I was lucky that he was home. When I knocked at the front door, he looked through the window and opened the door. The inside of the house was dark except for the kitchen. He showed me the way to the cellar stairs. Downstairs I found all six men digging earth from under the front of the house, behind the brick wall. Two bare lightbulbs cast an eerie light on the scene. They were working feverishly to shovel the earth into empty grain sacks they had piled at the corner of the cellar.

Jakob came over to me, his face full of sweat. He looked very tired. "Bezio, this work is too hard for you." He was always protective of me. "Go back to the camp. You will be able to visit mother in the Ghetto. The six of us will do the job. Aron has it all figured out."

I also knew that Jakob didn't want me to be there because it was risky to be in that house. In case of discovery, everyone would be killed--just like it had happened to Clara and her friends. He wanted me to survive. I listened to Jakob carefully and thought that he was right. He wanted me on the outside, near mother, to attend to all these things while he worked to build the bunker.

Before I left, I saw that many sacks filled with earth were piled on the cellar floor ready to be dumped into the empty well in the backyard. If not for this well, unused for many years, we would have not been able to dispose of the earth, and the bunker couldn't have been built. When the men were ready to dump the earth, Alus Schwartz would hide outside in the front to be on the lookout. If Alus saw anyone walking on the street, he would signal the others, who would immediately stop carrying the earth.

I said goodbye to all, hugged Jakob, removed my armband and left the cellar through its rear door. I headed briskly toward the camp, jumped over the fence, crossed the yard, and knocked at the door. The person who slept closest to the door opened it, surprised to see me. "Where have you been?"

I lied easily enough. "I went to the Ghetto to see my mother." I couldn't tell anyone about our bunker. I went directly to my bunk and thought with pleasure about the bunker.

It took more than three weeks for Aron and the others to excavate the area of all the earth. They worked at night and slept in the attic during the day. Then the difficult task was to build the structure. First, Aron had to find the sewer and connect it with the bunker. Since he had no sewer pipes, he built a pipe from four 2 x 4's, which he connected to the sewer line. He made a funnel shape and above it built a wooden toilet.

Aron then proceeded to dig two four-foot-deep cisterns, where water would accumulate when it rained and snowed. His idea to dig two cisterns under the sitting and sleeping area was ingenious. For Ivan to deliver pails of water for such a large group of people would have been impossible. In times of rain and when the cisterns would overflow, excess water would accumulate under the wooden floor. Part of the floor was removable so we could gather the excess water with pails and pour it down the toilet. But in times of drought, Ivan had to bring down a few pails of water just for drinking and cooking.

Aron's next step was to put down a wooden plank floor and to build the entire structure. The walls, ceilings, and the toilet enclosure were made out of wood with supporting wooden columns in between.

The toilet was two steps above the floor so it could be tilted and flushed down with pails of water. A wooden seat and a door for privacy were installed. Next to the toilet a curtain was put up to enclose a 2 x 2-foot area with a basin for washing.

Aron's next task was to tap into the electric line before it reached the meter in Ivan's house. Since the bunker would use substantial amounts of electricity, it could have been an indication to the authorities that someone other than the owners lived in the house. Electricity enabled us to have a dim light--five bare bulbs hanging from the ceiling.

Next, Aron built a brick and cement stove, 3 x 3 feet, to accommodate the large kettle for cooking our foods. Also he installed a small metal oven in the rear of the stove. Then he ran a gas pipe from the stove to the gas line before the meter, so that the meter would not register excessive use of gas and cause suspicion. He built a few shelves near the stove for utensils and for the scale we used to weigh food.

Aron extended the house's chimney down to the bunker. The sewer and the toilet were the source of our fresh air (you can imagine how fresh it smelled), and the chimney helped as an exhaust for the stale air. The chimney was also a means of communication in case of danger. A long wire with a bell on the end ran through the chimney from the kitchen to the bunker. Whenever a neighbor would visit or another situation might endanger us, Ivan pulled on the wire in the kitchen, and the warning bell would ring in the bunker. We would be totally silent until the bell signaled that the danger had passed.

I visited Ivan's house a few times while the bunker was being built. Watching Aron work was very encouraging. He had everything planned every step of the way in the building process. He smiled and laughed a lot and sang while he was working.

When the walls, floor, and ceiling were finished, Aron built a row of wooden planks along the 30-foot wall. Here everyone would sit during the day and sleep at night. Originally, there was space for sixteen. But later, when others arrived, there was not room enough. Eventually, a loft was built above the first sleeping space, and a few bunks were added between the stove and the toilet. Twenty- nine more people came than we had planned for--a total of forty-five souls.

To remove the earth and to build the bunker, part of the brick wall was removed. When the bunker structure and inside work were finished, five feet of earth was deposited around the bunker--on the top and the side facing the wall to the cellar. The walls facing the street and the sides needed no dirt "padding."

Aron's last job was to build an entrance to the bunker from the cellar. A 2 x 2-foot square entrance was made from the corner of the cellar. It led into a five-foot tunnel that opened into the bunker. The cellar entrance was covered by a concrete plate, which was covered by earth and then again by straw. A layer of straw over the entire cellar floor camouflaged the entrance to the bunker. Whenever Ivan entered the bunker, he had to dig up the earth and pick up the concrete plate. For all practical purposes, we were entombed in this hiding place.

Aron started building the bunker at the end of January 1943 and finished in April. Aron did most of the work, and the others helped him. We all knew that it was a race against time--before the liquidation of the Ghetto and the end of Jewish existence in Drohobycz.

One day when he was digging under the house, Aron found a mezuzah. This is a small container, usually metal, with a parchment inside on which Hebrew prayers are written. The Torah commands Jews to put mezuzahs on the doorposts of their homes. "It's a good omen," Aron showed the mezuzah to Jakob. "You will survive."

But Aron must have had private doubts that the bunker would survive. He felt that its location was dangerous. It was in the city and close to other houses and Gentile neighbors, who would be eager to tell the Nazis if they had any suspicions or saw something unusual. Aron did not plan to move his family into our bunker when it was finished. But he considered our bunker as an insurance in case his bunker in the Ghetto was discovered.

Mr. Kaczmarek, the manager of Mr. Schwartz's candle factory, knew that the bunker was being built. He let Ivan stay away from his job so that he was able to get additional supplies as the need arose. Ivan also had to be around the house to cover up the hammering and sawing noises during the building process. He would walk around outside the house with a saw or hammer in his hand, pretending to do repairs and to build the fence.

At the end of April 1943, the bunker was completed, and Aron returned to his family in the Ghetto. Mother, Jakob, and others totaling 15 people entered the bunker. I was still in the camp.

Liquidation of the Ghetto

End of April 1943

We were hearing rumors about the Warsaw Ghetto liquidation and uprising. Now we knew for sure that our Ghetto and all Ghettos in Poland would soon be liquidated.

Almost all of the Jews of Drohobycz had been taken away. I was one of the few survivors still working in the labor camps. The other survivors had gone into hiding, but nobody knew for sure how many they were or where they were. Everyone knew that the end was approaching.

Spring filled the city. The apple and cherry trees were blooming. From the windows of the camp, I watched children playing, people tending to their gardens, and peasants carrying fruits and milk products to the market. It was a beautiful time of the year for everyone but the Jews.

One day late in the afternoon after work, I removed my white armband and went to the Ghetto. I was going to the Kupferbergs' little grocery store, as Jakob had directed. The store was on a street near the Old Synagogue, the tallest building in the Ghetto. Most buildings in the Ghetto had no front doors--they had been broken down by the German police during the raids. Garbage was everywhere. Broken furniture and other debris gutted the streets. Only a few people walked the ghostly streets. The apartments stood empty, forlorn.

I passed by the Old Synagogue, standing in the midst of ruins. Its doors were ajar, so I stopped to look inside. It was an empty shell, ruined and dirty. When I had attended services there during the High Holidays, hundreds of Jews sat on benches, worshipping. Now the benches were gone. The holy ark where the Torahs were kept was gone too, and the walls were broken and filthy. I looked up at the high ceiling. Sunlight streamed through the stained glass windows, which were still intact.

I left the synagogue feeling sad, anxious and uneasy in the Ghetto. I didn't want to waste time because I had to see Mr. Kupferberg. Jakob had told me that he was an important party to the bunker. The money he would pay to enter the bunker would be used to pay Ivan.

Mr. Kupferberg's store was very small; only a few people could fit into it. You walked down a couple of steps to enter. He usually had only a couple of sacks of grain, sugar, rice, a few bottles of oil, and a couple of breads. He bought his supplies from Polish farmers, which was legal since there was no law against non-Jews entering the Ghetto. Inside the store it was always dim and dark--a single lightbulb dangled from the ceiling. I had visited the store only once before to buy candles.

As I approached the building, I noticed that the store was closed and that there was no entrance to the upstairs except through the store. I squeezed my nose against the window in the wooden door, trying to see if anyone was there. The store was empty.

I knocked several times on the peeling wooden door. No one answered, but I would not give up. I kept knocking and pounding on the door, waiting and listening, then pounding some more. After about five minutes of hard knocking, Mr. Kupferberg opened the door a crack. He looked surprised--and frightened. Gruffly he told me, "The store is closed."

"I come from Jakob Mayer," I answered, knowing what the name would mean to him. He turned his piercing eyes on me, looked me over carefully, and opened the door to let me in.

Mr. Kupferberg was a slim man with dark skin and graying bushy hair. He wore baggy pants and a wrinkled shirt; a jacket that was too big fell over his shoulders. "I'm Jakob's brother with news for you," I continued. I looked around the little store. Its windows were shuttered, the shelves completely empty except for a few empty bottles. A pile of brown papers for wrapping was neatly stacked on the floor. In the middle of the counter stood an old scale with different sized weights on its side. The air was thick and smelled of stale grains and bread.

As my eyes got used to the dim light, I noticed stairs in the corner of the store. Mr. Kupferberg led me upstairs to the apartment where I found the rest of the Kupferberg family. His wife was sitting next to the stove. She was slim with dark hair combed to the back. She had a very friendly demeanor, passive and quiet. Her eyes showed curiosity as she acknowledged my presence with a "Hello" and a smile.

Their son Mundek was about 13. He was quiet and had a sad face, but his look was very intense. He was slim with blond curly hair and sat at a table next to his sister Berta, a pale girl of about 16 with straight blond hair. Mundek and Berta kept looking at me.

Their little living quarters were more organized than other homes in the Ghetto. The stove held several pots, and the table had a tablecloth. The Kupferberg family didn't look as distressed as others in the Ghetto because they had money and food. Mr. Kupferberg was in control of the family and they trusted him.

I knew that the Kupferbergs coming to the bunker was very important to us. Ivan was waiting to be paid again; the four hundred American dollars they would pay to enter the bunker should satisfy him.

I stood at the door and told them, "Jakob says that the bunker is finished. He wants you to come tonight because the Ghetto may be liquidated any day now. Here is the address of a house outside the city where the bunker is located. A man named Ivan will be waiting for you. Knock three times on the front door, and he will open the door for you." From my many experiences walking outside of the Ghetto, I added, "Walk briskly, in pairs, and do not talk. If you see anyone on the street, don't approach Ivan's house."

The family stared at me, surprised. They didn't know me. "I'm Jakob's brother. You can trust me."

Mr. Kupferberg looked me over and smiled. His wife and children also looked at me with envy that I worked and moved around freely. "None of us have been outside the Ghetto since we came here," Mr. Kupferberg said. "We have a hiding place in the apartment."

All of the Kupferbergs seemed to stare at me as I talked. During the past two years since the Germans had arrived, I had grown up. At fifteen, I wore Jakob's navy double-breasted suit. I was proud that it fit me well. At work I was managing an entire table of brush workers and here I stood giving instructions on how to get to the bunker. I noticed that Berta was looking at me as if I were a man.

When I left the Kupferbergs' apartment, I walked the short distance to my mother's apartment. She was already in the bunker with Jakob, so I knew the apartment would be empty. I was hungry and hoped that some food remained. I found some grains, added water, and put on the gas stove. While the grains cooked, I filled a basin with water and washed my hands and face.

Then I heard a quiet knock on the door. Wondering who could possibly be visiting me, I opened the door. In front of me stood a beautiful girl about eighteen years old. She had black hair and a pretty face and figure. She smiled at me. "I saw you through the window when you were coming to the house. My name is Sara. I live upstairs and I want to talk to you."

I told her that I work in the camp and that I was in the apartment just for awhile. As I stood in front of her, she came closer, reached over to me, and kissed me on my lips. Then she turned slowly and left.

I had never seen her before, but I knew that there were Orthodox Jews living upstairs. Among them were Rabbi Avigdor, Chief Rabbi of Drohobycz, and some members of his family. His son was with me in the camp. I knew that Sara must be hiding somewhere upstairs and that she was lonely. She needed to reach out, to talk to someone, maybe love someone. Sara also knew that the end was coming. She wanted to know someone who could help her. My thoughts were running wild--should I take her to the bunker? How could I? My family would be angry. How about Ivan? He wouldn't go for it. I was sorry for Sara.

A few days later on a Sunday morning German soldiers and Ukrainian police cleaned out the Ghetto. They entered the Ghetto from all sides, flushing out every house. Some people escaped into camps. Others were not so lucky. Everyone caught was doomed. They were put on trucks and taken to Bronica Ravine, where they were shot. The police kept on returning to the Ghetto to break every door and window. They also dynamited many buildings. The entire Ghetto area was in rubble. At the end of April 1943, the Ghetto in Drohobycz ceased to exist.

At the Statishe Werkstaten more people arrived. Many came from the Ghetto. The majority were men, few women. The factory was going full swing, and my brush making department was excelling its previous production. Most of us were single, others widows and widowers, and most had lost all of their families. Tension was high but few despaired. There was always hope that somehow, through some miracle, one would survive. That feeling prevailed all the time to the end.

The Germans moved all workers from the camps to new sleeping quarters. They took one whole block on Garnekowska Street (literally, Potmakers' Street) and closed it at both ends with wooden gates and Ukrainian guards on the outside. They emptied the buildings so that all of the workers from the remaining labor camps could sleep at these new quarters. Garnekowska Street was outside the Ghetto, closer to the refineries and other camps, including the Statishe Werkstaten, where I worked.

Every day after work we marched as a group to our sleeping quarters. Each morning the guards opened the gates, and every group would line up separately to march to its camp.

The liquidation of the Ghetto and the tight control over our movements was a sign that the end for Jews in Drohobycz was approaching. Two months later, in June of 1943, early one morning the Germans arrived at the Garnekowska Street sleeping quarters. They shouted for everyone who worked at the Statishe Werkstaten to line up. Everyone who worked at my camp was put on trucks and taken to Bronica, where they were killed.

Escape to the Bunker

End of April 1943

    Several days after the liquidation of the Ghetto, I was at work when a supervisor at the labor camp interrupted my brush making. "Bezio," he spoke close to my ear so others shouldn't hear, "a man is waiting to talk with you. Downstairs by the front door." I felt all eyes were on me as I got up, trying not to hurry, and walked downstairs. It was an eerie feeling to be working in my gymnasium, the private school I had attended before the war. The building had many wonderful memories of students and teachers, who by this time had perished. Now all of the classroom walls had been knocked down and each floor was a single large room. Instead of students bending over their books, Jews bent over the brushes, toys, and shoe polish they made for the Germans.

    In the hallway downstairs I found Ivan waiting for me. He took me to the side of the empty hall where we could talk without anyone overhearing. Ivan looked very well dressed in his leather jacket and gleaming black leather boots. Our conversation was brief.

    "Bezio, Jakob sent me to take you to the bunker. Meet me in front of the house with the garden adjacent to Boryslawska Street at 8 o'clock tonight. Hide in the garden, and when I whistle, you come out, and we'll walk to my house." I nodded, and Ivan turned and walked out the door. No one had paid much attention to the fact that I spoke to a very well-dressed Gentile, who looked a little like a Gestapo man.

I ran upstairs back to my job, not meeting the questioning eyes of the workers at my table. I knew the time had come to leave and go underground, maybe forever. This is the last time I will be seeing these people, I thought. The beautiful young girl who always wore the blue dress was being courted by the young college man, who was one of our supervisors. I watched them always talking to each other with intense and loving looks. Would they survive? I felt very lucky to have a place to hide, but I knew I must be careful not to let anyone suspect I would be leaving the camp.

That evening in my sleeping quarters I opened the small suitcase where I kept my personal items. I saw the picture of myself wearing the white armband. It had been made in the camp by Mr. Kurtzer, a friend of my family, whom the Germans assigned to make I.D. photos of all workers. Mr. Kurtzer watched over me when I arrived in the camp and helped me to move from the difficult work in the carpentry department to the brush factory. He didn't have any children, and he liked me a lot. When I sat on the wooden chair for the I.D. photo, Mr. Kurtzer had snapped another pose of me with the white armband showing, and a few days later he gave me the photo as a gift. (The photo is on the cover of this book.) Now I put the picture in my pocket. It was the only thing I took with me before escaping to the bunker.

That night was clear but very dark. For the last time I jumped over the high fence. I landed in the garden of a two-story white house facing Boryslawska Street, where I was to meet Ivan. I lay on the ground and didn't move for several minutes. The lights were on in many rooms of the house, and I could hear voices. I listened intently, trying to figure out what language the people were speaking. A few minutes later I saw a shadowy figure behind a curtain reach out and open a window wide. Now I could hear distinctly that the voices were speaking German. I had jumped into a garden owned by a Gestapo man! I lay motionless, my heart beating fast. Then I moved slowly, crawling on my belly toward the shrubs close to Boryslawska Street, where I would wait for Ivan.

Now I could hear distinctly the Germans talking and laughing. I heard the clinking of wine glasses and the sound of their plates and silver. They had radio music on and they sang along.

I waited for Ivan at the edge of the garden next to the street. He had promised to come at 8 P.M., and I was half an hour early. As I waited, my thoughts ran wild. Maybe he wouldn't come. Maybe the Germans would discover me. I was scared. Calm down, Bezio, I told myself. I put my face against the wet grass and breathed quietly, listening to the music coming from the house. Soon I crawled closer to the street, and I waited in the bushes.

At last I heard footsteps coming in my direction, then whistling in rhythm to the footsteps. Ivan was on time as he promised. I picked myself up, stepped into the street, and met Ivan face to face. When he saw me, he whispered, "Bezio, do not talk to me. We need to turn around and walk in the opposite direction-- toward the city center. Behind me is walking this man who is a secret Gestapo agent."

The streets were completely empty. Ivan was moving fast, and I walked in step with him. After walking a few blocks, Ivan murmured, "We are going into a Ukrainian work camp to get away from the secret service man who is following us."

I trusted Ivan, but I was surprised at this move. Was it possible that Ivan was taking me to the camp-- to the dreaded Ukrainian farmers who killed my uncle? Worse, could he be taking me to the Ukrainian police? I had no choice but to follow his instructions. So I said nothing, put my hands in my pockets, and walked beside him trying to imitate his carefree step.

When we approached the camp, Ivan told me, "Don't talk in there. They may recognize that you are not Ukrainian." This was a volunteer camp for young Ukrainians who did physical labor for the Germans. Ivan was also a volunteer a few days a month.

A tall, slim man sat on a stool guarding a large, heavy gate blocking the entrance to the camp. Ivan greeted him in

Ukrainian, "*Yak idiet*?" ("How are things going?") It
sounded to me as if they knew each other. "I need to get in
to talk to my friends," Ivan continued. "Please open the
gate."

The man obliged and we came into the large yard.
Before the war, this had been a house where several doctors
had their offices. Now Ukrainian workers slept in the
house. Several men milled around the yard talking. Ivan
approached one of them. After greetings, he engaged in
small talk, asking for someone he knew. I stood next to
Ivan without saying a word. It was dark, and no one could
see my face. Ivan had told the man that I was his cousin.
As Ivan talked, he watched the street to see if the secret
service man passed. We both noticed the man as he walked
past the gate, which probably meant he was satisfied that we
were not Jews, but Ukrainians from the camp. Now Ivan
knew that it was time to leave.

After a few more minutes of talking and laughing, we
said, "*Dobryj Notch*" ("Good night"). Behind us I heard
Ivan's friends still laughing as the guard opened the gate and
we walked into the dark and empty street. Now we turned
away from the city and walked briskly toward Ivan's house
and the bunker.

As I walked, I wondered about the beautiful clear
spring night. How could it be so beautiful when Jews were
being taken away and killed? How could the earth go on as
if everything was normal? I saw my labor camp from afar,
where all those who worked with me remained to be

doomed. They had nowhere to go to hide. They had to work and wait. I was lucky I had a very slim chance for survival.

I felt as if I were a soldier at war, surrounded by enemies. Rescue seemed thousands of miles away--and very remote. You sit in the trenches knowing that people around you are killed and that any minute you may be killed, too. But you live from day to day, eat, joke, argue, even sing. And you hope that through some miracle, you will be rescued and survive.

Ivan and I walked past the house where I used to live and my aunt's house. Gentiles lived there now. The city was clear of Jews except for those in the five labor camps. After the Ghetto was liquidated, about a thousand Jews remained in the camps.

As we approached Ivan's house, he whispered, "Go to the rear of the house, Bezio, and wait until I open the cellar door. It will be safer if we don't enter the house together in case neighbors are watching."

I stood against the back of the house for a couple of minutes, listening intently for any noise or sound coming from inside. I knew that people were there already. But the only sound I heard was a grinding noise from a nearby factory. Otherwise the night was silent. At last I heard the turning of the key, and the steel door opened.

As I entered the cellar, the smell of earth and straw filled my nostrils. I touched the cold stone wall and stopped. My eyes turned to the faint light coming down the stairway from upstairs. Ivan closed the door behind me.

By now my eyes had gotten used to the cellar. I saw that what had once been a cement floor was covered by earth with straw strewn on top. Without saying a word, Ivan reached for a shovel and went to the corner of the cellar near the northern wall. As he dug the soft earth, he turned and said, "You see, this is the entrance to the bunker, Bezio. Those bastards will never be able to find out that Jews are living here." He kept on digging and talking to me, careful not to dirty his shiny leather boots. After a few minutes, the shovel scraped the cement cover--two by two feet in size. Carefully he removed the excess dirt with a wisk broom and lifted the cement plate with his strong, muscular arms. A light came up from the hole.

As I stood watching Ivan, I heard footsteps in the house upstairs. It was Mrs. Bur, his wife. "Bezio," Ivan said, "I have several large breads upstairs. Come up and help me carry them down." He took large steps toward the stairs, and I followed.

We entered the kitchen, where Mrs. Bur stood over the stove. She wore a dark skirt and light blouse. She had light brown hair and a round, pretty face. Her demeanor was unfriendly. I said "Hello" but she didn't respond.

The kitchen was painted white and sparsely furnished. Everything seemed very clean. In the middle stood a large table and a few chairs. In one corner was a large brick stove with a brick hood and a gas pipe connected to the outside.

In the opposite corner was a white wooden closet for dishes, where breads were also stored. While I gathered breads from the closet, Mrs. Bur left the kitchen. She seemed very uncomfortable in my presence.

The house had also two bedrooms with many windows all around it. I later learned that the Burs really never considered the house as their own. Mrs. Bur spent a lot of time with her family in the village, while Ivan stayed in the house during the week when he worked in the factory. They both came from large peasant families from a village called Stebnik about five kilometers from Drohobycz. When they married--maybe a year before--he was 20 and she was 24. After their marriage, Ivan decided to go to Drohobycz to seek work. He found a job in the candle factory, and they moved into the house that had belonged to the Schwartzes.

Later we found out that Mrs. Bur was very much against building the bunker. Her brother was a policeman in the Ukrainian police. But Mrs. Bur, who was four years his senior, loved Ivan. She loved him so much that she went along with the scheme of building a bunker under their house and risking their lives in the process.

Mrs. Bur felt like the majority of the Ukrainians, who had no love for Jews. No one in their families had any idea that Ivan and his wife were hiding Jews. It was obvious that Mrs. Bur never wanted to get involved in hiding Jews and was very critical of Ivan for doing it.

Ivan and I left the kitchen with six large round dark breads. We tossed the breads down the entrance to the bunker, and I jumped inside. Ivan followed me. Here I was in the finished bunker! The air was so hot that, as I looked around, I saw everyone dressed only in underwear. My mother rushed to greet me, crying with joy and relief. "Bezio," she hugged me, "at last you are here!"

Ivan ignored everyone and walked over to Jakob, who had followed my mother. With his usual smile, Ivan announced, "Jakob, I brought you Bezio." He told all who gathered around him about the secret policeman who had followed us and our visit to the Ukrainian work camp. He bragged about his having outwitted the mighty German Empire.

While Ivan told Jakob and the others about our walk to the bunker, my mother sat down with me on the plank of wood assigned to me. I took off my suit, shoes, and clothing down to my shorts.

I looked around me, seeing the bunker for the first time. I had seen only the cellar and the plans. Now it was real and people were actually living here. On top of the planks of wood were blankets and pillows that we slept on. Carefully I folded my clothing and put it under my head. I lay down and fell asleep immediately, ignoring all the noise around me.

About an hour later I opened my eyes to see planks of wood over my head. It took a moment for me to realize that I was looking at the ceiling of the bunker and that at last I was here. Next to me sat Alus Schwartz, eating his portion of thick barley soup. Alus and I were the same age. He was tall, thin with blue eyes and a long nose. But the thing you saw first when you looked at Alus was his ready smile.

We knew each other from the labor camp. After the first hunt he disappeared and went into hiding. Later he joined his father and helped Aron and Jakob build the bunker. He looked at me with a smile. "Bezio, welcome. I was waiting for you to arrive."

It was midnight, and the bunker was busy. "Why are you eating now?" I asked Alus.

"We are up at night and sleep during the day so people from the street shouldn't hear us. You'll soon get used to it."

Alus was six feet tall and had to bend when he walked in the bunker. He had to watch out not to crash into the light bulbs also. But he seldom walked. He sat in his assigned spot next to me. I tried to get off my bunk bed but I couldn't. There was so little room to move around. The bunker was only ten feet wide, and the stove, shelves, and beds took up most of the floor space. The pathway to the toilet was only a foot and a half wide, and now Mrs. Schwartz, Alus's mother, and Mrs. Bergwerk were busy distributing barley soup to everyone.

I lay across from them and watched. Mrs. Bergwerk was a short, stocky woman about forty. She had large strong arms, and she moved very quickly, ladling the barley soup from a kettle into an assortment of bowls and tins. Mrs. Schwartz carefully weighed each bowl on the scale that Ivan had provided and handed the bowl to the next person in line. Everyone received exactly the same amount of food--not a drop more or less, so there shouldn't be fighting. These two women had complete control over cooking and distributing the food.

The bunker was intensely hot. I was too excited to eat my ration, so I handed it to Alus, who devoured it in one minute. "Alus," I complained. "I can't take this heat. I will die from it."

"You'll get used to it," Alus replied with a broad smile on his face.

I decided to go the toilet. I walked slowly, barefoot, on the narrow wooden path to the other end of the bunker. I opened the wooden door and marveled that it also had a wooden toilet seat. It was really a bench with a hole in the middle. As I stood over the toilet, cool air hit my face. It felt good. I stopped perspiring; the foul sewer air felt refreshing.

Suddenly a wave of nausea hit me, my head ached, and I felt dizzy. I knelt over the toilet and vomited what I had eaten that night. I sat down on the toilet to rest. After a few minutes I came out, picked up the metal pail, and dipped it into the cistern for some water to pour down the toilet.

As I walked back to my assigned space, I tried not to stare at all the undressed bodies--fat, skinny, tall, short, old, young. I had never seen so many nearly naked people. They were sitting, lying, talking, and sleeping--everyone in their underwear. We were sixteen people altogether. I knew only a few, those that had built the bunker and the Kupferberg family.

On the wooden platform where we sat and slept, every four feet a pole supporting the ceiling separated each family or group. I lay down on my space and closed my eyes. My mind raced as I thought about all of the people I'd left in the camp. My friend Paul, who had gone to school with me before the war, was slim, intelligent, well mannered. Ever since his parents had been taken away, we'd been close. He always liked talking to me evenings after work. Since our sleeping quarters were cramped, we stayed on at the work area until we were ready to go to bed. I hadn't been able to tell Paul I was leaving.

I thought about Sara and about how desperate and frightened she was after the liquidation of the Ghetto, when I met her at the sleeping quarters of the labor camp.

My cousins Genia and Helen were most on my mind. After Ivan had arranged to meet me and take me to the bunker, I thought to have Genia and Helen come along. But I had no way to get in touch with them since they were in Herawka camp. Here I'm lying in hiding, I thought, and the others are out there with nowhere to hide.

I opened my eyes again, adjusted my pillow, and watched Mrs. Bergwerk and her son Manek scrub the large steel kettle. Everyone was relieved that the cooking was over because the stove made the heat unbearable. Amazed, I watched Mrs. Schwartz polish every spoon, dry the bowls, and clean the stove. She was a *ballaboosta* (a very good housekeeper) and cleaned the bunker's tiny kitchen as if it were her home after a party.

Alus saw that I was awake. "Bezio, what are you thinking about?" he punched my arm lightly. "Don't be so serious. At last we are here."

I didn't answer him. Alus was lucky to be with his parents and two sisters, I thought. But there were problems. How long were we going to have to stay here? And would Ivan continue to bring us food?

Ivan's Love Affair

The slim, attractive blond in the bunker had a pretty face. She was about thirty years old, medium height. She had light skin, red lips, and blue eyes. Her light golden hair was combed to the back, and she had a pony tail. I marveled at her beauty. Her name was Fay, and I imagined her behind the curtain as she frequently washed herself in the 2 x 2-foot area in the corner next to the toilet.

Fay and her older sister Sala, both single, were newcomers. They arrived in April at the same time with Itzak Shoenfeld, who came with his two sisters. They had paid Ivan hundreds of American dollars.

Before entering the bunker, Fay and Sala had lost their entire families. Shoenfeld's wife and child had also been taken away. He was in his mid-thirties, with red hair, white skin, freckles, and a long protruding nose. Shoenfeld had a good sense of humor and smiled often. He looked to be an amiable, carefree man, though in those days none of us were carefree any more.

They took up their spaces on the bunks, and Itzak Shoenfeld placed himself right between the two sisters-- Fay and Sala. He seemed to have no inhibitions about having sex with both of them. Life on the other end of the bunker only 15 feet away was different. There the families behaved "properly."

Several days after they arrived, Ivan opened the bunker and brought our supply of barley. He spoke a few words with Jakob and at the same time looked at Fay, the blond younger sister. She sat at her space wearing only panties and her bra--all of us were in underwear because of the heat. Her legs and breasts and the profile of her slim face were outstanding. Ivan didn't pay much attention to Jakob, who was holding money to pay for the barley. Instead, he proceeded toward Fay's bunk.

Itzak was lying down talking to Sala so as not to interfere with whatever was about to take place between Ivan and Fay. I watched Ivan smiling. Then in a loud voice he announced that the bunker would be open for a couple of hours. A sigh of relief--because the opening from the cellar brought in cool air. After several minutes, Fay exited the bunker. She went upstairs to be with Ivan. We knew that Mrs. Bur was in the village with her family.

I decided to put on my pants and go up into the cellar. It was a treat to smell the house and fried potatoes that were cooked upstairs. I would approach the cellar door facing the back yard, put my face against it, and glimpse the moon and stars through the cracks. It was a precious feeling to look out into the vast darkness.

Then I lay on the straw-covered earth and waited for Fay to return. I watched her descending from upstairs with a basket of cheese, meats, and bread. She didn't notice me where I lay in the corner of the back cellar. Then I knew it was time to rejoin everyone in the hot bunker because Ivan was about to come down to close the entrance and cover it with earth and straw.

Ivan kept on digging up the cover and opening the bunker frequently. Fay went upstairs at least twice a week, and I was always happy to get into the cellar for fresh air. At times Ivan brought down a few breads for us. He was enjoying his relationship with Fay, which benefited us too. Because of his love affair, we hoped that he would not turn us in to the Germans or abandon us. Our only fear was that Mrs. Bur should discover Ivan's love affair. It would be the end of Ivan and all of us in the bunker.

Returning to the overheated bunker was not easy for me. I removed my pants and shirt, folded them carefully, and put them under my pillow. Because of the change of temperature, I felt even hotter than before. Many people fanned themselves, but some lay still, looking up at the wooden ceiling above us. I could smell the meat that Fay was enjoying with her sister and Itzak. The smell of meat didn't really entice me, but I thought about the bread they were eating and imagined how nice it would be to have a piece of bread.

I closed my eyes. Lotka started to sing a Yiddish lullaby, and I fell asleep. Some time later my mother awakened me to have breakfast--black coffee and barley.

New Arrivals

May 1943

Here we were--the three remnants of my family, the Schwartzes, Bergwerks, and Kupferbergs, who came in recently and whom I knew. Hersh Ekstein and his wife Rose had been staying in Ivan's house during the building of the bunker, hiding in the attic. I found Mr. Ekstein sitting in his underwear, expressionless. He was a short, slim man in his early forties. His eyes were deeply set, and he didn't look strong to me.

His wife Rose approached me next morning as I was passing their bunk to get to the toilet. "Bezio, can I talk to you?" she asked in a low voice.

I turned to look at her. She was a slim, frail, small woman. Her hair was combed to the back, and she had a pale, sad face.

"Please sit down next to me," she said. "I need to talk to you."

They both moved over to make space for me right in between them. Then she continued, "Bezio, I wonder if you have possibly seen or heard about our boys. You probably knew them. Balek is sixteen years old and Mitek eighteen. They were in the Ghetto and later disappeared."

She talked and cried at the same time, wiping her eyes with a handkerchief. "Maybe they escaped to the forest?"

I looked at them, realizing how they both suffered here in hiding without their children. Then she reached for my hand and touched it gently.

I answered, "There is a good chance that they have escaped into the forest or into one of the camps. You must have hope that they are alive."

Mr. Ekstein didn't utter a word. A few minutes later I left to sit on my bunk next to Alus.

The liquidation of the Ghetto brought a lot of anxiety for the few Jews who remained in the camps and for those in temporary hiding places. Some Jews were hiding in basements or attics in Gentile homes, but usually the Gentiles made it clear that the arrangement was only temporary. These were good-hearted Gentiles who wanted to help but were afraid to be discovered and didn't want to risk their lives.

The Badjan family consisted of Grandma, mother of Muniek Badjan, who had befriended the top Gestapo members who later killed him in a hunting outing; Muniek's wife Janka and their three-year-old daughter Mushka; his sister Celia and her husband, who were the Galicas; and their three-and-a-half-year-old daughter Anulcia. In total the family consisted of four adults and two children. There was nowhere in town that this large family--especially with two children--could have been hidden.

They found out about Ivan's bunker through Engineer Backenroth, who was liked by the Gestapo and managed their Jana camp. Ivan hung around that camp to find Jews with money. Backenroth struck a deal with Ivan for a hefty price to let the entire Badjan family, who were hiding temporarily in other places, enter our bunker.

The night when the Badjan family arrived Ivan came down. He walked over to Jakob and said, "We have here an important group of people who will arrive soon. They are six members of the Badjan family including two children. Jakob, I want you to make room for them."

We knew the Badjan family well, and we knew that they had been influential in town. But two young children could cause a calamity; the Germans had discovered many bunkers and other hiding places because of crying children. But we really had no choice in this matter; the family was arriving soon.

When they arrived, I lay on my bunk and watched them enter the bunker. Grandma came in first. She was an obese woman, who hardly made it through the entrance. Mr. Galica followed, a heavy-set dentist with a friendly smile. Next was his wife Celia. Janka Badjan, the widow, came in last with both children.

Jakob greeted them, made room for them, and they settled in with all of us on the communal bunk.

The Badjan family was influential with Ivan. He brought them special foods from Engineer Backenroth, who was still in Jana camp. Special care had to be taken with the children, who behaved well. At times they cried, but they were given a lot of attention from all of us.

Now there were twenty-nine people in a bunker built for sixteen. The air became thicker and hotter, and the noise got louder.

The Radio

It was more than two months since I had entered the bunker. We were totally isolated from the outside world. Our only contact was with Ivan, who dug up the dirt in the corner of his cellar, lifted the cement plate, and lowered himself into our underground hiding place.

Ivan's usual task was to bring a sack of barley, a bag of imitation coffee, and paper for the toilet. Sometimes he brought a couple of large round breads. Whenever he brought supplies, Ivan would tell us news about world events and happenings in town. We were especially anxious to know if there were labor camps still left in Drohobycz and what was happening on the eastern front.

Because of our great anxiety about our fate, all of us were getting restless and irritable. We knew that the Russians had defeated the Germans at Stalingrad, but we didn't know how far away they were from us. We depended on the Russian victories and the advancing Russian army to liberate us.

Sometime in June we all decided that anyone who had money left would chip in and we would ask Ivan to buy us a radio and a large map of Europe that we would put on the wall. We wanted to follow each battle to see how close--or far away--the Russians were.

At that time anyone who owned a radio had to register it with the German police; and in order to buy a radio, you needed a permit from the German police. The Germans controlled radios because they didn't want people to know how badly they were doing on the eastern front. Therefore, people kept their radios hidden and listened to them only in their cellars.

As usual, it was my brother Jakob who negotiated with Ivan. The next time Ivan brought a sack of barley, Jakob approached him. "You know, Ivashko," as he called him, "we must have a radio. We got together one hundred dollars. Would you go into town and get us a shortwave radio? You can buy it only with American dollars. Someone will be willing to trade his radio for a fortune like this."

Ivan smiled--as he usually did--and took the money. "Jakob, you know me well now. I know how to get things. Do you want a gun? I can get it for you."

"No, no, we don't want guns. We only need a radio."

Ivan said in a serious tone of voice, "I know, I know. You need it and I will get it. It's not a big deal."

Jakob warned him to be careful, but Ivan smiled reassuringly. "Don't be so nervous--you are too nervous. I know how to handle things." Ivan put the money in his pants pocket and wiggled himself into the opening with his lean, athletic body--fast like a monkey. He closed the cement plate and covered it with dirt until next time.

Everyone was very enthusiastic about the prospect of having a radio--everyone, that is, except Mr. Schwartz. "I never listened to the radio before, so I don't need the radio now," he said. "God talks to me through the prayers. We must believe in Him." But the rest of us knew that after food, the radio was next in importance because it would be our lifeline with the world.

More than two weeks passed while we waited impatiently for Ivan to return with the new supply of barley and the radio. Usually he would open the bunker every few days. Now anxiety befell us. We spent sleepless nights worrying about Ivan's fate. We knew that we were doomed without Ivan--our very existence depended on him. Our last sack of barley was getting smaller and would last only a few more days.

At last, early one morning we heard footsteps in the house. We recognized the steps of Ivan's wife, whose name we never knew; we called her Burowa, which means "the wife of Bur" in Ukrainian. Her footsteps continued for about two hours, and then all was quiet. Since Ivan and his wife had a home in the village, she visited the house infrequently. At times we heard trucks passing by, but otherwise silence prevailed.

Another whole week passed. What had become of Ivan? It was three weeks since his last visit. At 2 A.M. on a Sunday morning, we heard fast footsteps above us. In hushed voices, we asked who it could be. The steps continued for about twenty minutes. Then all of a sudden the bell attached to the wire, hanging out of the chimney, rang twice. This meant that Ivan was about to open the bunker.

Everyone was ecstatic. We hugged each other and sighed with relief. We listened intently to the sound of the shovel as Ivan cleared the dirt, then lifted the plate, and lowered himself into the bunker. He stood with a radio in his hands, his face lit in a broad smile, and his light-blond hair over his forehead. "Here you see I got," he boasted. "Anything Ivan wants, Ivan gets."

We got around Ivan and hugged him, knowing that he liked to feel important. My brother Jakob told him, "When we will all be liberated, we will carry you on our shoulders into the center of town and show everyone what a hero you are!"

Ivan handed the radio to Jakob and sat down on the edge of our bunk bed. He looked tired as he told us the ordeal he had been through. "I went to the Rynek, where people are selling used things. There is a tall, well- dressed man selling clothing. I think, he looks like a person who has a radio--elegant and cultured. First, I approach him about the clothing. Then I say, `You know, Mister, I would like to buy a radio. I have dollars to pay for it. It will make you rich.'

"The man looks at me suspiciously, but I show him the money--looking around to see if anybody sees it. Then he tells me that he has a Telefunken shortwave radio, exactly what I want. `OK,' he says. He gathers his things and asks me to go home with him. At his home, he goes into the cellar where he keeps the radio hidden and brings it up and plugs it in. It plays beautifully. I check it well--longwaves and shortwaves. It is OK. I tell him that I can spend the hundred dollars on it, and the deal is made. Afterward, he asks me to have a vodka with him, so I stay at his house until it gets dark.

"I ask him for a sack, so I put the radio in it and carry it over my shoulder. I am walking fast toward home when I see two Gestapo policemen coming toward me. They ask me what I am carrying in the sack, and I tell them wood. They make me open the sack, and then they take me to headquarters to interrogate me all about the radio."

We seemed, all of us, to hold our breaths as Ivan told his story. "They ask me about my address and I tell them the Stebnik house where my wife lives--not this place. They put me in jail and two days later they go to my wife and tell her that I am in jail because I have committed a big crime.

"My wife quickly tells her brother, who is a Ukrainian policeman, and he comes over right away. He gets in touch with other people, who bribe the Germans to have me released with the radio. You are lucky to have this radio, Jakob," he smiled.

Ivan was happy. He walked over to his girlfriend Fay, kissed her on the cheek, and gave her a look. Then he squeezed himself into the entrance of the bunker. His girlfriend Fay followed him, and they spent the evening together in the house. A couple of hours later she returned with a basket of food. Ivan covered us again, and we heard the sound of the earth falling over the cement cover.

The radio was a Telefunken shortwave--a large, brown portable with longwave and shortwave dials and an eye that told you if your station was on target. We all crowded around it. We plugged it in, moved the dial, and to our surprise it played. We kept on turning the dial until we found a Russian station that had news broadcasts that described the locations of each army and the battles that were fought. Living underground, we got fantastic reception from Germany, Russia, England, even as far as Palestine. We most often listened to the Voice of America, the British Broadcasting news, and news in Polish. We also listened to the German news and enjoyed their description of their defeats on the fronts. But most important, we listened to the frequent and explicit reports from Moscow. We followed every movement of the Russian armies, especially the army in the southern Ukraine, which was moving in our direction.

We placed the radio on a shelf over Mrs. Koenig's bunk, and hung the map on the wall beneath the shelf. Mrs. Koenig did not welcome the crowd around her bunk, but no big arguments occurred because to listen to the radio was very important, and she knew it.

To make sure that the radio would not get damaged or abused, Mundek Kupferberg was assigned to attend to it. Only Mundek was allowed to turn on the radio and adjust its dials. Mundek was a slim boy of thirteen, very good with his hands, and extremely bright. He taught us young people how to play chess. He also was the barber who cut everyone's hair. Therefore, we had confidence in him to take care of the radio.

Since the radio worked on electric tubes, we used it sparingly. We knew that it would be difficult to have it fixed if any of the many tubes would burn out. Sometimes there would be arguments when the radio was on. We who wanted to listen to it wanted everyone to stop talking. There were a lot of "Shhhshhh's!" as the eastern front was getting closer to us. We would listen every half hour to the news bulletins even though they were repetitious of the same reports. We needed reassurance and hope. To listen to news of the Russian victories on the eastern front was more important to most of us than even eating.

To save the radio, we limited our listening to the news. But there was one exception, and that was the broadcast from Palestine every Friday night of the Jewish Sabbath service. Mr. Schwartz, who was the most observant Jew among us, would take his prayer book and follow the prayers. At that time the bunker would be completely silent. Most of us would lie or sit on our bunk spaces, some embracing, others crying with emotion. To hear Hebrew prayers and the beautiful chanting had most of us in tears. Here we listened to our people free in the Holy Land, praying to us entombed underground with a small possibility of survival. It gave us hope and courage.

The radio played an important part in our survival. It kept our hopes alive until liberation.

Aron's Odyssey

One night in May of 1943 around ten o'clock Ivan rang the bell twice, the signal that he was opening the bunker. We heard him digging and then lifting the cement cover. To our astonishment, Aron Shapiro entered, followed by his wife Malka and their small son. Aron, who had planned and built our bunker, was back. Aron jumped toward Jakob and hugged him. Aron's clothes were wet, his face unshaven, his eyes bloodshot. He looked exhausted. Aron's wife stood behind him, holding their son in her arms. Lotka Schwartz in the space next to me moved aside and asked Malka to sit down.

"Jakob, the Germans discovered us. We have many problems--it's a mess." I could hear the frustration, anger, and pain in Aron's voice. I got up and stood next to Jakob so I could hear better. The bunker was quiet; everyone strained to hear his story.

First Aron told us of the bunker he had built for his family under 8 Kowalska Street, the building in the Ghetto where he lived. "You see, I built your bunker after I finished mine. I built a large bunker for my family and relatives--about 80 people, and we accumulated a year's supply of food. Our bunker was the envy of every Jew who

heard about it. We had everything--even a shower made
from a car radiator. After the second action, everyone looked
for a place to hide. We had the best chance." Aron paused
and gave Malka a sad look.

"The Germans knew there was a bunker somewhere in
the Ghetto, but they didn't know where. When they
liquidated the Ghetto, they tried very hard to find the bunker,
but during the weeks before we had worked hard on an
escape exit to the sewers.

"So it happened today. We heard the Germans
breaking every part of the building above us. They threw a
hand grenade down the basement where our entrance was
camouflaged. When the smoke filled our bunker, we were
coughing and had to leave--we couldn't breathe. So we all
entered the sewers. I told everyone to meet across from
Ivan's house in an abandoned factory building." Aron
frowned, remembering the panic and confusion.

"Many were lost in the sewer system and eventually
they were picked up by the Ukrainian and German police
when they came up on the streets. But twenty of us are
waiting in the building across the street. Now I'm leaving
my wife and son with you. I'm going into the forest with
the others to build a new bunker, and when it's finished,"
again he looked at Malka, "I'll be back to pick up my
family."

My heart beat fast watching Aron in such distress.
Malka was a young woman in her late twenties with a round,
full, pretty face. She, too, was exhausted and sat quietly

next to her son. She kept her eyes down, looking up only to watch Aron as he spoke to us.

Jakob handed Aron a pair of pants and a shirt, and Aron washed his face and changed. Lotka Schwartz helped Malka and her little boy. Because of the heat, Malka removed her dress and folded it neatly. Then she lay down with her son next to Lotka.

I sat down in my space--next to their little boy, who had fallen asleep as soon as he lay down. I watched him sleeping peacefully. He had black, curly hair and long black eyelashes.

I looked up and motioned for Jakob to come near. "We are in a lot of danger," I whispered. "There are twenty people across the street. Tell Aron to take them away from here soon, or we will be discovered."

"I can't do that," Jakob shook his head. "Aron will have to make his own decision. I trust him--he knows what to do."

Aron stood silently in front of the stove. He stared at the shelf above the stove, where there were four large breads. He turned to Jakob and looked straight at him. "May I take the breads for all of us?" I knew that he didn't have to ask. Even though we rarely got bread from Ivan and it was a delicacy for us, we didn't mind parting with the breads for Aron's sake.

"Take anything you need," Jakob told him.

Aron bent down to where Malka lay. He hugged her, then kissed her on the cheek. He looked intently at his sleeping son. Then he hugged Jakob and murmured, "After I finish the bunker, I will be back for my family."

Aron crawled into the exit. Ivan followed him and closed the bunker.

Late one evening in July 1943, we heard Ivan's footsteps upstairs. Two rings of the bell silenced the bunker. Usually when we ate, people talked loudly even though Jakob kept reminding us to be quiet. Ivan opened the bunker and came inside followed by Aron. Aron looked good. His face was clean shaven, and he wore high boots. He and Malka embraced, a long hug. Malka wept with relief to see him again. There had been no word from him since he had left.

Aron picked up their son and hugged him. "I missed you both so much! Now I have finished the bunker in the forest. Everyone has settled in, and we can be together again." Aron smiled broadly. He hugged Ivan and Jakob several times, enthusiastic and optimistic as we were used to seeing him.

Aron and Jakob sat down next to me to talk. "You see," Aron said, the words he always used to begin a story, "when the Germans discovered the bunker I had built in the Ghetto, only twenty people survived. Four of my brothers and some of their families and others survived, and I could not abandon them. They depended on me to plan and build another bunker. We all need to survive." He spoke with emotion, emphasizing his words with sweeping gestures of his hands. "We will survive or perish together."

Then Aron told us what had happened after he left us two months before. "That night we left the building across the street and walked in pairs until we left Drohobycz. We entered the deep forest near Podbusz, ten kilometers from here. My brothers and I knew the area well because we lived not far from there and as children we had played in the forest. Years later my brothers had bought furs from the forest ranger who lives not too far away.

"We found a spot where the forest was thick, and we lay down among the trees. Everyone was exhausted and slept through the night. The next morning we realized we had a problem. We had no tools for building and no utensils for cooking. We had only our bare hands and a few knives.

"My brother Szymon and I approached the small cottage where the forest ranger and his wife live. When he saw us, he was startled. `What are you doing here? I thought there are no more Jews around!'

"I explained to him that we have money and need his help. We begged him to help us, and finally his wife had pity on us and agreed to sell us a shovel, some grain, and utensils for cooking. She also promised to continue to sell us food.

"It took us awhile to build the bunker. Most of the time we dug with our bare hands. We built the bunker like a hole in the ground, and we camouflaged the top with sticks and grass. We built a small stove inside the bunker and made a chimney from a tree trunk to hide it." Aron paused and looked around. Everyone was quiet, listening to his story.

"During the day we sleep, and at night we cook. We carry the water from the creek nearby. Our toilet is a hole in the ground inside the bunker. Life is difficult, but we have hopes to survive. In the beginning it was very hard, but now it is better and safer. Therefore I come to pick up my wife and son."

I thought that Aron seemed confident and enthusiastic even though the conditions he described were harsh. But he felt more comfortable outdoors than confined in a bunker like ours. As he worked on the bunker with us, Aron had often said that he couldn't live in an underground bunker like ours--at the mercy of a Gentile--because he needed freedom and control.

Yoshua Sheinfeld had listened intently to Aron's story. Yoshua was slim, medium-sized, in his early thirties, bald with piercing brown eyes and a sad face. He was a recent arrival in the bunker and had no family. An intellectual and a loner, he was on edge and unhappy in our environment. Yoshua was the only one who wore a tight black bathing suit--we all wore underwear--because the oppressive heat bothered him a lot. He was excited when he heard Aron's story. When Aron stopped talking, Yoshua pushed toward him. "You have a place in the woods where I can join you? I don't want to be here. The heat is terrible, and I don't like Ivan." He spoke in Yiddish so Ivan could not understand.

"There is a good possibility that we may be discovered here."

Aron looked at Yoshua. I noticed always that Aron's face showed his goodness, compassion, and enthusiasm. "Come with us," he told Yoshua.

It was almost midnight when Aron picked up his son, again embraced Jakob, and left the bunker followed by Malka, Yoshua, and Ivan. Ivan closed the bunker behind them.

We continued with our everyday night life, preparing for breakfast.

Five months later, December 1943

At least during the winter it wasn't as hot in the bunker. The air coming through the toilet was cool. We had enough water. The cisterns were full, at times overflowing. One night about ten o'clock (morning for us), Mushka, the little three-year-old Badjan girl, had a nightmare, and her screams woke us.

Soon there were two rings of the bell, and Ivan opened the bunker. He crawled in looking tired, without his usual smile. Ivan approached our bunk, where Jakob lay asleep. I was awake and nudged my brother.

"Jakob," Ivan began, "we have a problem. I have in my house five people. They claim they are Aron's family. They know about the bunker, and they insist on getting in."

I knew what that meant--something had happened to Aron.

Ivan, Jakob, and I went up to the cellar to see those who had arrived. In situations like this, if anyone knows about your hiding place, you can't refuse him entrance; you always let him in. We found two of Aron's brothers--Yoske and Szymon, two of Szymon's teen-age sons, and Elie, a young man of twenty. Jakob knew the brothers. All five sat in the dark corner of the cellar. They were barefoot, their pants and shirts ripped, and they smelled terribly of feces. Before they told us anything, we brought pails of water into the cellar and clean underwear. The group washed and changed. I told Ivan that they really are Aron's family and we need to help them. He agreed hesitantly, realizing that he must go along with it.

That night Aron's brothers sat on Jakob's bunk telling us their story. Everybody listened. Szymon, the older brother, was about forty, dark-haired with black burning eyes and a muscular body.

Szymon started to talk but broke into sobs. Jakob put his hand on Szymon's shoulder as he cried great gulping sobs. After several minutes Szymon was able to speak. "We had a difficult time in the forest," he began, "because it was a problem to get food. Finally Mrs. Zuk, the forest ranger's wife, had pity on us. It was an awkward situation. Her husband didn't want to help, but she had a good heart. We paid her, and she agreed to supply us with corn, barley, bread, and potatoes. Her husband didn't want to get involved with us, and he even scolded her for helping us get food. We would go to the house when he wasn't around and pick up food that she had prepared for us without his knowledge."

Szymon continued, interrupted only by Yoske, who filled in details, "We cooked at night and slept during the day. During the day no one ventured outside the bunker. It was always dark in the bunker although a little light came through the wooden twigs that covered us. Many of us developed diarrhea, and we used the large hole that we had dug in the bunker for our toilet. There was, of course, no privacy. By the end of November, the first snow fell, and we had to be very careful not to go out so we wouldn't leave footprints in the snow."

Szymon looked at Yoske, and we could see the pain on their faces. "Mr. Stern, the intellectual and a very sensitive man, became severely ill with diarrhea. He was too embarrassed to use the hole so frequently, so he kept on going outside, and he left footprints in the snow leading to our bunker. Aron tried to stop him, but no one could hold him back. We were all sick and frightened.

"Some farmers noticed his footprints. Three days ago early in the morning Ukrainian and German police surrounded our bunker. They were shooting all over. For a while it became very quiet and the shooting stopped. Nobody moved, but Yoshua Sheinfeld, the man who came from your bunker, was curious to know what was going on. He lifted the twigs and stuck out his head. The police shot him through the head. He was killed instantly, dropping back into the bunker."

Yoshua Sheinfeld had left our bunker because he couldn't stand it here, I thought. And now he is dead, and we are still alive. The bunker was absolutely silent as Szymon went on with his story.

"Aron realized that we were doomed. Thinking fast, he told me, Yoske, and my three sons to get into the hole full of feces." Szymon looked up at Elie, "Elie Heilig jumped in also to save his life," Szymon added, struggling not to cry, "so there was no room for my oldest son." And now he glared at Elie, "He took my son's life. We all lay on top of each other. Aron quickly covered us with wood and twigs, and then he opened the bunker. All fifteen people, including his wife and child came out.

"Realizing that for sure the police must know about his bunker building activities, Aron ran away from the bunker so he wouldn't be caught and questioned, and the police shot him on the spot. They put the others on a truck and took them away to be killed. Aron couldn't even try to save his wife and child because he knew the child would have cried in the pit."

Szymon's face showed great anguish as he continued. "The police climbed into the bunker and removed all our belongings including the pots. They spent a whole day returning with other peasants to marvel at the bunker's construction. All the time we lay inside the pit, listening to it all. We heard two peasants saying that the Germans had shot Mrs. Zuk, the forest ranger's wife. Somehow they traced the cooking pots to her. They dragged her screaming from her cottage and shot her for giving food to Jews. But they didn't touch Mr. Zuk, who insisted he had nothing to do with it.

"Many hours later when night fell, we got out. We had no clothing to change to. To keep warm, we huddled together. It took us two nights to get to you. We had to walk nights only, hiding behind houses and barns. When we reached Ivan's house, we hid in the back behind the dry well Aron had told us about. I knocked on the front door, and Ivan opened it, very surprised to see me."

When he finished his story, Szymon sobbed intensely for what seemed like a long time. Jakob looked around. Everyone watched, silent. Jakob told everyone to squeeze themselves closer together on the bunks to make room for Aron's family.

That made thirty-five of us in the bunker, including two young children.

Close Call

December 1943

A loud knocking at the upstairs door woke me and also Recia Schwartz lying next to her brother Alus. She whispered to me not to wake the others. "Did you hear the knocking?"

I didn't answer her. I raised my head and looked at the faint light from the bulb over the toilet--our night light while we were sleeping. It was 2 P.M. upstairs.

"Bezio, I'm afraid," Recia whispered. "I don't like this."

I noticed some heads rising in the distance, but they all lay down and went back to sleep.

Recia was a slim, frail young woman of 21. She had a small face with large brown eyes and curly black hair. She was the conscience of the Schwartz family and of everyone else in the bunker. She worried about everyone in the bunker, especially about the children Anulcia and Mushka. Recia played with the little girls and helped to feed them and wash their clothing. She talked about the people she watched being taken away when she was hiding in the attic of the candle factory. Here is one of the many poems she wrote in the bunker:

1944
In the dark hole away from civilization
Forty souls wake up simultaneously,
Cut off from the world,
Hiding from the arm of the executioners.

We sit in this hole many months,
Everyone frightened for his life.
The single ring of the bell means danger,
That our time has come.
At this time we lose our faith,
Afraid we will join our departed brothers,
The thousands who were taken to the camps
To enormous suffering, and to death.

Recia was not only compassionate and sensitive, but also extremely bright. She spent most of her time writing poetry and a diary about her stay in the bunker.

The loud knocking continued upstairs. I knew it came from the front door. Then one ring of the warning bell shattered our night silence. When we were awake, many times some of us would hit the bell to quiet feuding people or stop family arguments. Therefore, many of us ignored the ringing of the bell. But this ring during the night silence was a genuine warning.

Now everyone was up, even the two little girls-- Anulcia, 2 1/2, and Mushka, 3. I could feel the tension in the bunker. None of us moved from our spaces; for a couple of minutes there was complete silence.

Then I heard walking with heavy boots all over the house. We could hear several people walking from room to room. Jakob quietly got off his bunk and moved silently down the row of lying and sleeping figures. In a low voice he reassured them, "Please be calm. Take deep breaths and hold onto each other." He told the Badjan family to take the little girls in their arms, to cuddle and rock them. The Grandma sat down and took Mushka in her arms and rocked her back to sleep. Anulcia lay awake and very quiet in her mother's arms. She was not yet three, but she knew and understood danger. I could hear deep sighs and the mumbling of prayers.

I sat up and listened and knew that there were visitors in Ivan's house. Jakob quietly climbed the stove to reach the chimney, so he could hear the voices upstairs. He came down after a few minutes and whispered, "Germans are here. Everyone stay calm. Don't move or talk, please. Our lives depend on your behavior."

Now even the last light was out. Silence prevailed. No one dared to talk. I just heard faint words mumbled by Mr. Schwartz, Alus's father, who prayed for us all. The sound of walking was loud and the moving of furniture was continuous. It felt like the house was being taken apart. I experienced a feeling of despair that I never had before.

My thoughts were terrifying. I saw myself being dragged out and taken away, probably to Bronica, where my sister Clara had been killed. It was cold outside. They will take us on trucks for the half-hour ride and shoot us and throw us into the pit, I thought. By now I knew what to expect. There were no secrets any more. The Jews who were being discovered in Drohobycz--and there were few by now--weren't going to labor camps any more. They were disposed of immediately right here.

Then I heard the breaking of the cellar wall. We were only five feet away from the Germans, separated by the five feet of earth Aron and others had packed in between the bunker and the cellar. Aron--surely a genius--had had the foresight to imagine what would happen if the Germans came to search for our bunker, so he surrounded it with five feet of earth.

My mind raced back to the day my father died, in 1937 before the war. It was a cold day in January on a Friday. I was playing outside with some neighbors when my Aunt Lipcia brought me into the house. My father lay on the bed covered with a white sheet. Then I went into the kitchen and saw the wet floor; they had just washed his body in the kitchen. I was nine years old. My mother dressed in a black coat and the entire family followed my father's body. My brothers and uncles carried his coffin for several miles, from our house to the cemetery in the freezing temperatures and high snow. It was an honor for the dead to be carried in this way rather than transported by horse and wagon. I was left in the house with a neighbor because my mother wanted to protect me, spare me from the long trip in the freezing cold.

Will I be spared again, I wondered? Or are we to be discovered?

Suddenly the knocking on one wall of the cellar stopped. We heard the heavy footsteps of several people walking over us in all directions.

Knocking started upstairs, this time directly over us. I gathered that they were ripping up the floors and banging with some objects. Loud knocking continued for a long time all over the house.

My mother lying next to me took my hand and held on tightly. With each blow above us, I felt a skip of my heart. I looked up at the ceiling, expecting a direct hit. Then with the next blow we heard a scratch at our ceiling. My mother's hand tightened, and I held my breath. A few more hits continued, and then all of a sudden they stopped.

Heavy walking continued again for several minutes. We continued to listen; no one talked or moved. After awhile we heard light, quick footsteps of Mrs. Bur followed by two rings of the bell--our all-clear signal.

Three hours had passed since Recia and I had heard the first loud knocking at the front door.

Jakob put on the light. We all lay in our spaces afraid to talk or move. I looked around me. Recia was in shock. She didn't move but sobbed. My mother still held onto my hand gently. Jakob told everyone to be quiet. I felt relieved but still terribly frightened. We knew that the Germans had been here, but we had to wait for Ivan to open the bunker to find out what really had happened.

Two rings meant that danger was over, but we were not ecstatic. Everyone talked in low voices. We were still scared. I turned to Alus, "Did you hear how close we were to being discovered? They were scratching our ceiling. One more thrust and they would have found us. A miracle! Why did they stop?"

"My father's prayers were heard," Alus replied. "He saved us."

I thought about the Germans. Will they be back? They are suspicious. Now they will watch the house and Ivan's movements. Delivery of food will be more difficult.

Late that night we heard Ivan's footsteps, and we anxiously awaited the opening of the bunker. At last we heard the digging of the earth at the entrance.

Ivan crawled in. He stood at the entrance, his face pale, anxious, and serious. No one spoke. Ivan started, "We had a visit from the Germans and Ukrainian police today. My wife was alone. They couldn't find you." Then he motioned to Jakob to come up into the cellar. Jakob put on his pants, and I followed him.

Ivan murmured, "I want you to hear the story from my woman. She refuses to come tell you herself because she won't go into the bunker. I'm going to tell her to come down to the cellar."

Jakob and I sat down on the cellar floor to wait for Mrs. Bur. We sat close to the steps that led to the kitchen.

Ivan and his wife came down immediately and sat on the middle step, where the light from the kitchen shone on their faces.

Mrs. Bur did not look at us but began talking immediately, "I heard a strong knock on the front door when I was in the bedroom. I came into the kitchen and looked through the window. There were two trucks in front of my house with four soldiers carrying machine guns. I realized immediately that we are in trouble." She talked haltingly, looking angrily at Ivan, who kept his head and eyes down. Her voice was firm yet uneasy.

"First I ran to the stove to pull the chimney lever that rings your bell in the bunker. Then slowly I opened the door, looking surprised as the Germans and Ukrainians pushed the door open and entered. They pushed me against the wall holding a rifle against my chest. A Ukrainian policeman screamed at me, `Where are the Jews? We know you have Jews in this house. Mrs. Flunt, your neighbor, came to the police station two days ago and told us that she saw several people in the back yard. You must have them here.'"

I looked at Jakob. A couple of days ago the Shapiro men arrived from the forest and were hiding in the back yard. That night they waited for Ivan to get home, and Mrs. Flunt had probably seen them waiting.

Mrs. Bur kept on talking, "`I have no Jews here,' I told them, and I started laughing. `My brother Michal

Kapek is in your police. Do you think that I'm going to hide Jews?'

"I opened all the doors, and they kept holding the rifle at my back. The Ukrainian policeman talked to me a little nicer now. `You tell us where the Jews are and you will not be harmed. Just tell us, we know that they are here. You can tell me, I'm your family friend.'

"`I have no Jews!' I reached for the shovel and handed it over to him. `Here, if you don't believe me, dig. Maybe you can find them.'

"My heart was beating fast. I was acting well, laughing loud, and saying, `Imagine--I hiding Jews, this scum. I'm glad that we got rid of them!'

"But they persisted. They sat me down at the kitchen table, still pointing the rifle at me. Then they called the soldiers from outside, who brought picks and shovels and other tools."

She leaned back and rested for a moment, still giving Ivan a dirty look. She still avoided any eye contact with Jakob and me.

"They started in the basement digging at several places. Then they were breaking the cellar wall in two places, finding only the dirt behind the wall. When they didn't find anything, they became furious and they again asked me to show the place where I was hiding the Jews. Then the German talked to the Ukrainian about something that included the word *grenade*. I felt that I'm going to die.

"The Ukrainian turned to me and said, `This is your last chance. Because we are going to blow up your house.'

"I laughed in his face." She was now trembling when she talked about it. "The Ukrainian gave orders to the soldiers to check the attic and the back yard. Then they started to lift the wooden floors all over the house. They used crow bars to lift the wood, then broke the cement underneath, and stuck the long picks into the earth underneath." Then Mrs. Bur moved down a step to be closer to us and continued, "You can't imagine how scared I was when they were digging down where you were, but I laughed all the time. I told them, `You people are crazy!' They were exhausted and showed some compassion for me. All of a sudden they stopped, and a German told the soldiers to leave. They left me alone in the kitchen. Then the Ukrainian policeman approached me and murmured with a smile, `We are sorry for this. Your neighbor must have been dreaming. We can't find any Jews here.'"

Mrs. Bur lifted her muscular right arm and crossed herself twice. "Christ gave me strength not to surrender. I will pray every day to God."

As I listened to Mrs. Bur, my heart was beating fast. I thought how brave she was.

All of a sudden she stood up, looked at her husband, and said to us, "If Ivan were here, he would have broken down, and we would all be dead by now."

She turned and walked upstairs into the house. Jakob and I returned to the bunker to tell everyone what had happened upstairs and how brave was Mrs. Bur.

More New Arrivals

April 1944

After Ivan opened the bunker, Jakob and I went into the cellar to cool off, as we frequently did. We noticed a pile of lumber stacked against the cellar wall. Jakob asked Ivan, "Why do you have all that lumber?"

Ivan murmured, "We are going to build another tier of bunk beds. We have more people arriving soon."

I noticed Jakob's surprised tone of voice, "Ivan, we are not going to able to live here with more people inside. We can't breathe as it is now. The air is too thick and hot."

Ivan picked up a piece of wood, handed it to Jakob and said, "We need to save as many Jews as possible. There are still a few hundred Jews left in the Jana camp. I promised several people to bring them here. We must make room for them."

Jakob didn't answer Ivan, but picked up one of the boards Ivan had piled in front of us, and handed it over to me to get it inside the bunker. I called down for someone to take the boards and place them on the floor under the bunks. They were all cut to size. Now we had the task of nailing them to the support poles, three feet above our bunks, enough room to sit.

Next evening Ivan came down bringing nails and a couple of hammers. Jakob, the Shapiro family, and I had the job to put up the next row of boards. It took us four evenings to finish the job.

The Galica family had sent Ivan to see Engineer Backenroth, a Jew still in the Jana camp. Backenroth gave Ivan foods to deliver to the Galicas. At the same time, Ivan made connections with those in the Jana camp who had some money and wanted to enter our bunker. All of them-- with one exception--paid Ivan in gold and diamonds.

Now the bunker's second tier was practically full of newcomers. The elite of Drohobycz had arrived. These were the remnants of our Jewish community who had survived in Jana, one of the last labor camps. Jana was a service camp for the Nazi Gestapo. The newcomers were privileged Jews, who worked as doctors, dentists, and pharmacists, or who had attended to the Germans' basic needs, like cleaning or gardening.

Among the privileged were Manek Zukerberg, his wife, his brother, and sister-in-law. Mr. Zukerberg, who was in his thirties, was a pharmacist, a short, stocky man with a round unfriendly face. He had worked for the Germans but became alarmed that they might kill him before they leave town. So he decided to enter our bunker with his wife and brother. Mr. Zukerberg had connections outside, and they provided special foods for him and his family.

At the same time as the Zukerbergs, Mrs. Haberman arrived with her son and her sister. Mrs. Haberman was

short, well-rounded, a pretty woman. She and her husband
had owned the largest jewelry store in Drohobycz before the
war.

Paul Hertzig and his wife Rose arrived a few days
later. He was the Jewish manager of the Statishe
Werkstaten, where I had worked making brushes, but he
managed to escape before my old camp was raided by the
Germans.

Hertzig, who had been a man of stature in the camp,
arrived at the bunker emotionally and physically sick. In the
past year he seemed to have aged 20 years. He was only 44
years old, yet the skin on his face was hanging, and his
arms and legs were terribly skinny. Hertzig was a gentle
man and the only one of the "elite" newcomers who
ventured down from the top bunk to sit with me. He liked
to tell me stories about his beautiful life before the war, how
his marriage was arranged by a meeting on a cruise ship to
Ireland. His wife, who was the daughter of a prominent
lawyer, was 18 years younger than he, and the war had put
a strain on their marriage. Since Mrs. Hertzig had some
diamonds left, she would give Ivan a diamond each time to
get meat, cheeses, and other good foods not available to us
old timers. Many times Mr. Hertzig and I played checkers,
chess, or cards. Each time he would come down to sit with
me, he brought for me a sliver of meat, cheese, or bread.
These morsels of food were a real treat for me and a great
generosity from a man who needed it for himself.

The last of the newcomers was a very beautiful 19-year-old woman named Genia. She had not had to pay Ivan anything, for he had invited her to the bunker to be his second lover.

The newcomers lay above us on the second tier of bunks. There was not enough space for them to sit up; they could only lie down. Aron had not designed the bunker for two tiers of bunks. We had planned for only sixteen people originally. Who could imagine that there would be forty-five people crammed into such a small underground tomb? The heat, which had been unbearable before, became even worse because more bodies had to breathe.

Life in the Bunker
April 1943 to August 1944

Potatoes

The bunk right behind the oven was the size of a bench, smaller than the narrow spaces we lay on. On the wall above it hung the map of eastern Europe and above that was the shelf where the radio rested. We often gathered around the radio to listen to the latest news and check the advancing troops on the map. To Mrs. Koenig, who lay on this bunk, we were invading her space.

Mrs. Koenig was a short, fat woman, who had arrived from a labor camp sometime during the spring. She had approached Ivan directly. She had money because she had owned a large shoe store before the war. No one knew how much she had paid Ivan to enter our bunker, but we assumed it was a lot.

Mrs. Koenig wore her long black hair in a tight braid around her round face. Her eyes were black like coal. Even though it had been several years since there was enough food for Jews in Drohobycz, Mrs. Koenig had double chins and that fleshy, well-fed look that many Jews had had before the Germans arrived. In the bunker's heat, she wore black panties and a black bra, her breasts protruding and overflowing. Mrs. Koenig had been assigned to this bench because she was too fat to fit into any of the narrow bunks we lay on. On the narrow bench across from our bunks, her ample flesh could overflow into what little space there was in our aisle.

She expressed great dissatisfaction with her resting spot because many of us gathered around it to listen to the radio and look at the map. Mundek used a blue pen to mark on the map the areas recaptured by the Russians. Alus and I stood in front of the map a couple of times a day to measure how far away the approaching Russians were.

One day during the summer of 1944, Ivan came down with a sack of potatoes. Potatoes were a real treat, a treasure, a change from the endless barley. Before the war, potatoes were a staple of our diet, but this was the first time in the bunker that we would taste potatoes.

I watched Mrs. Schwartz and Mrs. Bergwerk, our cooks, discuss the fate of the potatoes. To cook them or to bake them? They discussed the pros and cons for a long time, and finally decided to bake the potatoes so as not to lose the skins. Besides, water was scarce. There had been no rain for weeks, and both cisterns were dry. Ivan now had the most difficult job of carrying water from a street pump. He carried a pail in each hand and brought them right into the bunker. We used the water only for drinking and cooking. Water now became more precious than food.

While the kettle of barley for dinner was cooking, Mrs. Schwartz and Mrs. Bergwerk carefully placed 45 potatoes in the oven. We would eat them the next morning for breakfast--one potato per person. After the potatoes had finished baking, they remained in the oven to keep them warm for breakfast.

The lights were dimmed for our night. Next morning the cooks announced that there will be no need to cook barley since we had lukewarm potatoes for breakfast. Everyone would get a potato and a cup of water. Mrs. Bergwerk opened the oven, gathered all the potatoes into a pail--and counted only 43. She turned to Mrs. Schwartz in despair. "We have only 43 potatoes! Someone has stolen two potatoes! I counted three times. Now two people will not have breakfast."

Loud protests came from all sides. "Who stole the potatoes?"

Jakob walked over to the bell and rang it once, silencing the outcry for only a few moments. A quiet voice spoke up. It was Ana, a shy fifteen-year-old girl. Even though she was my age, I didn't know her well because she never talked to us. She lay on her bunk across from the radio and stared at everyone with her large brown eyes.

"I know who ate the potatoes," Ana said in a low voice. "I woke up when I heard some noise. I sat up and right in front of me I saw Mrs. Koenig opening the oven. She reached in and took out two potatoes. Then she lay down on her bunk. I saw it all."

Mrs. Koenig sat on her bench, her legs crossed, and her body leaning back against the wall. Her face was flushed, and her hair was in disarray. As she looked at Ana, tears rolled down her fat cheeks. She mumbled out the words, "I was hungry." Then she got off her bunk and jumped into one of the dry empty cisterns. She lowered her head inside and sobbed. It was the coolest place in the bunker.

Everyone gathered around, shocked, screaming at her, "What are you doing inside that thing? Get out! You're not supposed to be in there. We keep our water there! You're making it filthy!"

After an hour, it took three men to pull her out of the cistern.

Drought

Dry holes in the ground were the problem. Tempers ran high. I watched the bodies lying flat on their bunks with pieces of paper in their hands, fanning. During the summer, the heat seemed endless, sickening. Because of the drought, the toilet wasn't flushed for days, and its foul smell filled the bunker at all times.

One evening Ivan came into the bunker wearing a white shirt with rolled-up sleeves. Perspiration ran down his forehead and down his unshaven chin. He walked up to Jakob and announced in a firm voice, "No one can use any water until we have rain." He turned to his right and left, repeating his order.

Mrs. Galica protested, "We need water to wash the children."

"You people are impossible!" Ivan shouted. "I will bring water only for cooking and a bit for drinking." He shook his head for emphasis.

Then Ivan went upstairs, leaving the bunker open. I took advantage of this by going up into the cellar. I sat down on the cool cellar floor. The air felt fresh and cool, a delightful feeling after the heat and stench of the bunker.

Half an hour later, it was dark outside. I saw Ivan opening the cellar door. He rolled in a large wooden barrel and placed it next to the door. Then he took two large empty pails and left. Within 15 minutes he was back with them full of water. He emptied the pails, left again, and kept on going and coming until the barrel was full. There was a pump on the street about two blocks away, and Ivan was carrying buckets of water from there. He risked the neighbors' suspicions with these many trips for water.

Late that night, Jakob, I, and some others went up to the cellar to fetch the water needed for cooking. We were responsible for making sure there was just enough in the bunker. The rest remained upstairs in the barrel.

The water shortage lasted several weeks. The heat and stench from the toilet became unbearable--and still we bore it--until the rain began and water filled our cisterns.

Lotka

At my end of the bunker, the Schwartzes and the Kupferberg families were close to me. Recia and Lotka Schwartz were gymnasium-educated and raised strictly by their parents. I lay between them. To my right, Lotka was singing Yiddish or Polish songs. She had a very good voice and remembered all the words. She sang all the time, repeating the same songs. Eventually I joined her many times, singing along. It made us feel good to sing, and others listened to the old songs with pleasure.

Lotka was 19 years old. She had a round face, black eyes, and black hair that curled round her face. Like her brother Alus, she had thin lips that were quick to smile.

Lotka was very sentimental, amiable, and gentle. She had a frightened look and was intensely concerned with the well-being of her family. Many times she screamed at her father, the religious man, or at her brother Alus. But most of the time she spent with a dreamy look on her face, singing---or screaming in pain.

Her spot was at the end of the bunker facing the entrance. She always watched the entrance, expecting someone to come or waiting for Ivan to open the bunker to give her fresh air. She showed impatience with her inability to be free. Lotka kept away from others in the bunker. After our meals, Lotka would start singing in a low voice.

Sometimes she would tell me about the school she had attended before the Nazis arrived. She would describe the food she had eaten, especially the chocolate tortes her mother had prepared for dessert. I spent a lot of time imagining the taste and delicate texture of those chocolate tortes! Lotka talked about the songs she used to sing at home. She would start with *"Tum balah laika"* in her soft voice, then change to *"By mir bis tu shein."* Many times I would join her in a very low voice. When others heard Lotka singing, the bunker would become silent. She had a touch of magic in her voice.

One day in March of 1944, Lotka noticed a boil under her left arm that kept getting larger and more painful. As the days passed, her pain increased, causing her to scream frequently. She covered the boil with pieces of fabric and continued to suffer. I felt terrible for her. All of the Schwartz family and others in the bunker were terribly upset, but there was nothing any of us could do for Lotka. We had no medicines, no aspirin, no ointments--nothing.

All of us at our end of the bunker fussed over Lotka. My mother's job was to get the washing bowl, where she would wash Lotka's used pieces of fabric, or rags, as we called them. After two or three weeks of agony, Ivan finally brought Lotka some aspirins to ease her pain. But the boil did not heal, and her pain continued. Ivan carefully watched Lotka and everyone else who was sick.

Typhus

March 1944

My mother's face was ashen and sweaty. She struggled to breathe, taking deep breaths. My mother lay next to me without uttering a sound. Now she turned her face to me, opened her eyes, and looked at me sadly. She was sick. She hadn't been eating much, only drinking the dark-tinted water we called coffee.

"Mom, why don't you eat?"

"I can't, Bezio. I'm sick."

I really didn't have to ask. Tonia Mayer, who was always energetic, looked exhausted.

She had weathered many misfortunes in her life. Raised in a small Polish town called Kozlow, she was one of five children. During World War I, she lost her mother and two brothers. She and her mother and another brother had escaped from their town to live in Vienna, Austria, during her teenage years. Then she came to Drohobycz, where her two sisters lived, and started a successful hand-knitting business. In 1926 she married my father Isaac, a widower with three children.

She was a survivor. I looked at her now so helpless and weak. Her stomach couldn't hold any food. Everyone around her gave her advice, but she knew best what to do. When I was a child, she would give me grated apples for stomach problems. Ivan had brought a load of green apples and left them on the cellar floor. My mother asked me to get her some. Carefully she peeled an apple, chopped it into small pieces, and ate it. She did this a few times a day. It took her several days to feel better. Slowly she ate barley again and regained her strength. During that ordeal she lost all of her hair. We found out later that she had had typhus.

The typhus spread in the bunker. Mrs. Schwartz became sick, and so did a dozen others. The typhus devastated all those who became ill, but the green apples on the cellar floor came to the rescue. Everyone who got sick ate the apples and was cured.

The Holy Man

I first met Herman Schwartz in Ivan's house. I knew that before the war he was the real owner of this house where we were to build the bunker. He was a thin, short man with a drawn skinny face. He was in his forties, the oldest of our group. He was muscular, and I noticed that he wasn't afraid to work. He had worked hard most of his life in his candle factory. That night in the cellar, he came over to me and asked if I have tefillen (phylacteries) for praying. Observant Jewish men put tefillen on their arm, hand, and forehead while they say the morning prayers.

"I forgot my tefillen, and I need to pray to God every day." His voice was worried, urgent. "When you come back the next time, Bezio, make sure to bring me the tefillen."

I looked at him, very surprised. We are here to build a bunker, I thought. Why would he think about praying? I promised that when I returned next time from the labor camp that I would bring them if possible.

Mr. Schwartz was persistent when it came to his religion. He told everyone to get him tefillen. He figured that someone would bring them for him; the more people he told, the better were his chances.

I arrived in the bunker in April 1943, and I found Mr. Schwartz with a pair of tefillen. It was Aron who came back from the Ghetto and brought Mr. Schwartz what he had been wanting so badly.

To most of us in the bunker, Mr. Schwartz was a nuisance when he got up earlier than others. He put on his tallis (prayer shawl) and tefillin and stood in front of his bunk bed, saying the morning prayers aloud. He blocked the pathway to the bathroom and stove. Most of us felt that he made our lives more difficult, but he was not ashamed or even considerate of others when it came to observing his religion. Mr. Schwartz cooked his own grain in the little pot--scorned by the cooks-- because he wanted to observe the laws of kashruth (keeping kosher) more carefully than he felt they did.

He continued his religious tradition when at times on Friday nights, he would remove all the light bulbs from their sockets because he wanted to make love to his wife on the bunk bed. (According to Jewish tradition, on Friday night, the beginning of the Sabbath, pleasurable and happy experiences need to take place.) This caused laughter, ridicule from many, and embarrassment for his daughters and son, but Mr. Schwartz would not bend. He prayed, he ate, and he made love according to his Jewish traditions as he saw fit.

Mike, the Horror Man

April 1944

Among the new arrivals was Mike Kleiner, whom we soon began to call among ourselves "the horror man." Mike was in his thirties, short and slim, with skinny arms and round shoulders. He had an unfriendly face and bullying eyes. He made it clear from the outset that he was not a nice person and that he was mean. Mike didn't talk to me--only to the Haberman family.

Mike Kleiner's eyes bulged out when he got angry, and that was very often. Life in the bunker was difficult enough before Mike arrived with the Haberman family. It was a mystery to me how gentle people, rich before the war, had got involved with Mike.

No one really knew Mike from before the war. Jakob told me that he must be an out-of-towner. Jakob knew almost everyone in Drohobycz, but he said that he had never met Mike before.

Mike arrived wearing a leather coat and boots. He looked very important--like the German secret service man who had followed Ivan and me in town. When Jakob approached him and told him where his space was, up on the second tier, Mike yelled out, "Don't tell me where to sit!" The veins on his forehead popped up and his eyes bulged.

Immediately Mike made it clear to everyone that he was the boss, the top banana, and that he would give orders to all. Now life became unbearable. Mike gave the order to have the lights out earlier, and he restricted the use of the radio. Since the radio was our important source of information and entertainment, Mike purposely would shut it off.

Jakob decided for the sake of peace and quiet not to challenge him. But Mrs. Koening, who was twice his weight, decided to take him on.

One Friday night when we listened to our program of prayers from Jerusalem on the BBC, Mike pushed himself through those of us who were listening and turned the radio off. Mrs. Koening, who was lying on her bunk under the radio, grabbed his arm and pulled on it until he gave such a scream that it scared all of us. This time his face got terribly red. There was no telling what would happen next. Mike walked away from the radio, mumbling to himself in pain.

One day Mike took on the cooks. He looked at the sacks of barley that were dwindling and he told the cooks to make less. "Add more water. It will make more soup."

Mrs. Bergwerk's voice was angry. "We are here for over a year. We know what and how much to cook. Don't tell us what to do. You eat all the extra foods with the Zukerbergs and Habermans, and you tell us what to do!"

She took Mr. Schwartz's little pot from the stove and hit Mike on the forehead. "Not my pot!" Mr. Schwartz screamed and rushed to grab it from her.

After being struck on the forehead, Mike fell on the bunk next to Lotka. He lay there asleep for several hours.

Mike's anger was continuous. He never smiled or showed any graciousness. He walked with clenched fists, always ready to fight. At times he carried a knife that he had brought from the outside. He was a terror that caused all of us a lot of pain.

For Jakob especially, Mike's behavior was very taxing. Since the beginning Jakob had organized our life in the bunker. He negotiated with Ivan about purchasing food. He advised Ivan how to approach peasants so as not to cause suspicion. Mike was disrupting everything and putting our lives in jeopardy. Everyone hated him but didn't know how to handle him. At last Jakob decided to ignore Mike and told everyone else to do the same. It was very difficult for all of us.

Alus

When I was in the Statishe Werkstaten making brushes for the Germans, I sat at a large table filling empty holes in the brush with bristles. One day I glanced up to watch a young man standing at one end of the large workroom. He was about 14, tall, slim, blond with blue eyes. He struggled with a large pile of wire on the floor, winding the wire onto small spools that we used at the table. Clearly he was new at his job and upset that it was so difficult for him to do.

At the end of the day's work I walked over to him and said, "Alus, you must find a better and faster way to wind the wire onto these spools. Why don't you ask Mr. Bender, our supervisor? He will show you how."

Alus nodded in agreement and left for home. It was at the time when we still lived at home while working in the camp.

Every day Alus stood alone, winding the wire onto the spools, not talking to anyone. He kept to himself most of the time, apparently in deep thought. Alus remained at the labor camp until the first hunt, but he never returned. I wondered if he had been captured by the Germans, but I didn't know who to ask.

I didn't see him again until eight months later, when Aron began to build our bunker. Alus was one of the six men filling the sacks of earth in Ivan's cellar. "Alus--what are you doing here?" I asked him.

"This is my house," he answered, surprised. "I left the Statishe Werkstaten during the first hunt and went to hide in the candle factory with my family. Mr. Kaczmarek, our employee before the war, hid me and my family. I decided never to go back to work at the camp, but to live in hiding in the back of the factory."

As I was leaving the cellar that night, Alus approached me. "Why do you go back, Bezio? Stay with us here."

"I can't," I told him. "I must go back to the camp to be near my mother. When the bunker is finished, I'll be back."

As I talked, Alus was bending over to fill the sacks with earth. Then he turned to me, and I saw his face in the flicker of a candle. He smiled at me, stretched out his hand, and hugged me. "I'll be back, Alus, and we will be together," I told him.

In April 1943 when I entered the bunker, I found Alus lying right next to my assigned place in the bunk. It was important to have someone your own age next to you, I thought. Alus showed an interest in me because he had the same needs as I did.

The day we got the radio, Alus had an argument with Mr. Ekstein. Alus insisted on listening to a Polish program broadcast by the BBC, but Mr. Ekstein didn't want to listen

to Polish. He carried on, "They are anti-Semites! They
didn't help the Jews!"

Alus agreed. "But it's my language that I understand
best."

I suggested that to settle the argument, we should listen
to Polish only every second day, and this satisfied them
both.

In the bunker, eating our daily ration of barley was a
ritual that was not very exciting. Such dull, bland,
unvarying food had no meaning, and I had no real hunger
for it. But Alus had an appetite and was always waiting for
the time to eat. As the months passed, Alus grew thinner,
and his long face became pale. He seldom left his space on
the bunk and watched everyone around him.

But Alus talked all the time. I had no choice but to
listen, and he was funny. He had nicknames for a number
of people. For example, he called Mrs. Koenig "the fat
one." The Shapiro boys he called "*Chiri Biri Bim* and *Chiri
Biri Bum*" because they had a Chasidic movement to their
walk. He called Bertha Kupferberg "the yellow one"
because she had a pale yellow complexion.

Playing cards and chess were Alus's hobbies, and he
insisted that I be his partner, so I obliged. He entertained me
and I laughed. He added humor to a sad, almost bleak,
hopeless situation whose outcome was unknown.

Many times Mundek Kupferberg, who liked to carve dogs and horses out of scraps of wood when he could find them, joined us to play chess. Alus enjoyed telling me stories, especially about his escape from the Statishe Werkstaten during the first action. He told me, "Everyone in the camp became very nervous that Friday morning. I didn't see you, Bezio. You were gone. I decided to leave very early and go to my father's candle factory because I knew my family was hiding there. I opened the back door of the camp building, ran through the backyard, and jumped over the wooden fence. I kept on jumping over all the fences, not to be seen on the streets. I never knew that I had so much strength to run through the fields and gardens at such tremendous speed."

After telling me the story again, Alus would tell me about the chocolate cakes his mother used to bake, the vacations he used to take, or how at seven years of age he was run over by a car and spent three months in the hospital. There were only two cars in Drohobycz, and Alus managed to get hit by one of them. His stories would end just before mealtime, when the bowl of barley would keep him quiet for awhile. Then he would tell another story or pay a visit to the radio to listen to his Polish program.

One early morning the floor of the bunker was wet because the rain had overfilled the cisterns. After weeks of drought, we were in the season of too much rain. I walked barefoot through the water. It was my turn to remove parts of the wooden floor and gather the water with a pail. I handed the pail to Alus, who carried it to the toilet and poured the excess water down the toilet.

But that morning Alus had an idea. He lay down on the floor and washed himself. I followed him, then Mundek, Manek, and the Shapiro boys. We had our morning bath together, laughing and splashing each other. Our underwear got wet, but we dried pretty fast from the heat around us.

Alus and I spent 485 days and nights lying and sitting next to each other. We exchanged fears, anxieties, jokes, laughter, memories, and vague plans for the future. We never fought because Alus didn't know how to get angry.

Ivan's Plot

May 1944

Those of us who had been in the bunker for over a year became thinner, weaker, and sick, like my mother and Mrs. Schwartz, who had typhus, and Lotka with her boil. Now Ivan noticed the differences in the physical condition of the oldtimers and the newcomers. The newcomers were stronger, heavier, and healthier. Ivan also knew that there were many Jews still in Jana who had money and needed to leave and hide.

One Saturday night Ivan opened the bunker. It was Genia's turn to go upstairs. Genia had found a space among my family and the Schwartzes. I used to look at her very closely. She had magnificent shapely legs, a narrow waist, and full breasts. Her face was oval with full red lips, light brown hair, and blue eyes. To me she was beautiful--more beautiful even than Fay, Ivan's first lover. Genia didn't stay in one place on the bunks. She was restless and moved around from space to space. She was very quiet and seldom talked. Since she had arrived, there was tension between the two rival lovers. Fay and Genia didn't talk to each other. But I noticed that Genia was going upstairs more frequently than Fay.

Ivan brought the newcomers packages of food for the money, gold, and diamonds he collected from them. We oldtimers were still eating barley most of the time. Jakob and I knew that we were running low on money to pay Ivan for food supplies, since most of the oldtimers and the Shapiro group had nothing to contribute.

On a Monday night in May 1944, Ivan opened the bunker. I was the first one to put on my pants and slip into the cool cellar. I lay down in the dark corner on the straw. All I wanted was to feel cool. A few minutes later Jakob lay down next to me. We enjoyed the cool earth under us and the stale, humid cool air of the cellar.

A while later we noticed Mr. Galica, the dentist, and his wife Celia crawling out of the bunker. Mr. Zukerberg, who followed them, was obese and had difficulty getting out. At the other end of the cellar, we saw the shadowy figure of Ivan sitting on the steps that led into the kitchen. None of them noticed Jakob and me, since the three of them walked directly toward the steps where Ivan was sitting.

Ivan started talking in a very low voice. Mr. Galica stood against the wall with his wife, and Mr. Zukerberg sat on the ground facing Ivan, who sat on the upper step.

"We have people who are here many months--over a year," Ivan began. "I think most of them are sick, tired, malnourished, and about to die." Ivan talked slowly, hesitantly. "It will be a long time until liberation, and the oldtimers will probably not make it. Look at Lotka, Mrs.

Mayer, and Mrs. Schwartz. They are all sick. They will only suffer and die." Ivan paused. No one uttered a word.

"They will infect others-- you and the children," Ivan continued. "I was thinking about it, and I want to share my thoughts with you. Dr. Frommer is still in the Jana camp. I will tell him to come over to look over the condition of these oldtimers."

Jakob and I lay motionless. Jakob put his hand on my mouth. I knew he meant for me not to talk or move. I couldn't believe what I was hearing because I had all the confidence in Ivan. He had worked hard with us to build the bunker. He had cooperated with all of us. Then he got me out of the camp, risking his own life to get me into the bunker.

Ivan cleared his throat and added, "It will be best to get rid of the oldtimers. I will go to the camp and bring the healthy Jews who will be able to survive. After one year underground, these oldtimers have had it. They will not live much longer."

Mr. Zukerberg, the pharmacist, asked, "What do you mean, Ivan? Explain to us what you want to do."

Ivan paused for a minute. Then he continued, "I'm going to the camp and talk to Dr. Frommer to tell him to come to the bunker with me to evaluate the oldtimers and take along lethal injections. Those whom he will find in bad shape, he will inject and put them to sleep forever. The dry well in our back yard is the place where I will dispose of the bodies. Then we will have enough room for the new, healthy Jews."

Mr. Galica, who had a very pleasant personality, said, "No, no."

Mr. Zukerberg said, "I don't know what to say."

To feel out what their reaction will be, Ivan repeated, "I will have Dr. Frommer come here and look over the situation. He will inject those that he finds to be sick or in bad condition."

Jakob and I slowly slipped unnoticed back into the bunker. We left Ivan and the other three in the cellar, still talking about Ivan's plan. Back in the bunker, we lay on our bunks waiting impatiently for the three to return and for Ivan to close the bunker. After a few minutes Mr. and Mrs. Galica came down into the bunker. Their faces were pale. They made no eye contact with anyone but took their places at their bunks. I saw them lie motionless.

Then a few minutes later Mr. Zukerberg came in. He was heavyset, his face was red, as was his bald head. He looked upset, excited, and nervous. I watched him climb to his bunk with difficulty, and I noticed his hands were shaking. I felt sick to my stomach seeing death again.

Jakob's face showed anger and fear. He put his finger to his lips to tell me to be quiet. We waited for Ivan to close the bunker. I knew that Jakob was going to explode. He and mother were the ones who conceived of the bunker in the first place, with the Schwartzes and Bergwerks, who also contributed with labor. The Kupferbergs contributed all their money. Now to be killed by lethal injection was unbelievable. And by a Jewish doctor, yet! It must have been a dream, I thought.

As soon as Ivan closed the bunker, Jakob stood up and went to the middle, where everyone could hear him. "Listen everyone. Be quiet."

Jakob's voice was level, but I could hear his anger. "I want everyone to know that all those of us who came in first to the bunker will be poisoned and thrown into the well in the back yard."

People cried out in disbelief and terror. "We will be given an injection by Dr. Frommer. Tonight this was discussed in the cellar, and by chance, thank God, Bezio and I overheard it. The Galicas and Zukerbergs know about it. They are the ones Ivan talked to about it."

Everyone was shocked and frightened. They all wanted to know details. I told over again what I had heard. Lotka, who still suffered with her boil, began to cry. "How can he do it? It is just like the Nazis. I won't let anyone, even Dr. Frommer, touch me."

Mr. Kupferberg, who was always very quiet, slammed his hand against the wall. "We are well," he cried out. "They don't have to poison us."

Then Jakob told everyone to be quiet. "Dr. Frommer will be coming in a couple of days," he said. "I have a plan for us to beat this thing. We are going to clean and scrub the bunks. Everyone will wash his clothes and change into the best they have. All men will shave and take haircuts from

Mundek Kupferberg. Women will wash and fix their hair, put lipstick on their lips and cheeks to look healthy. When Dr. Frommer will see us healthy looking, he may not want to kill us."

Everyone agreed that Jakob's plan was the best way to dissuade Dr. Frommer and Ivan from disposing of us.

Some of the newcomers expressed their outrage when they heard of Ivan's plan. The Galica family was friendly, and Mr. Galica spoke reassuringly, "Don't worry. Nothing will happen to you. Ivan got crazy for money."

Mr. Hertzig, whom I knew from my labor camp, was pacifying Jakob and me. He was a gentleman and had held a high position in an export company before the war. Mr. Hertzig kept on telling me, "We stand with you, Bezio. We will not let you or any of the others be injected with poison."

But I knew better. If Ivan wanted to get rid of us, he would find a way.

Jakob called the Shapiro brothers, Aron's two brothers, to sit at our bunk. Yoske in his early thirties had large biceps, and his body was athletic. He sat down next to Jakob and me. He had black curly hair and black fiery eyes. "Jakob and Bezio," Yoske told us, "we must defend ourselves. Nobody is going to poison us. I will not allow it. Sure Ivan wants to bring more Jews with money into our bunker. He sees an opportunity to get gold and diamonds. He forgot that Aron and all of you worked hard to build this bunker. The Russians are getting closer to us every day. We may have a chance to survive if Ivan lets us live."

Jakob and I listened to him carefully. Then I said, "We must be very careful not to make Ivan angry. He tries-- anything to make money. He has ideas that are at times stupid."

Yoske scowled at me. "Bezio, he wants to get rid of us. He is serious. It's true that we are in his hands, and he can hurt us. But let's not forget that he has all those newcomers and his two girlfriends among us. We will fight. We will die fighting."

I knew that Yoske was frightened and angry as all of us were. The entire bunker was in turmoil. That evening the cooks prepared our breakfast but very few ate. I went over to the radio to listen to the Russian news program. The Russians were approaching the old Polish border. The Germans were in retreat, but still they were a few hundred kilometers from Drohobycz. We had still a long wait to be liberated.

I could smell the burned barley. It wasn't often that the cooks burned our barley. They hadn't watched the kettle that night--who could blame them?

My mother lay next to me. She turned her head in my direction. Her hair was growing back after the typhus. She was still pale but seemed much stronger. "Don't worry, Bezio," she patted my hand. "I feel good. I'm sure Dr. Frommer will find me fit to live. I know that Dr. Frommer will be fair and we should not become hysterical."

Eventually Ivan realized that we knew about his plans. He opened the bunker a couple of times only to invite one of his girlfriends upstairs. On a Sunday night he told us that Dr. Frommer will be coming next day to check those who were ill, especially Lotka, who suffered excruciating pain.

Next morning the oldtimers got busy. Everyone went to the enclosed corner to wash up. Mundek Kupferberg was cutting hair for everyone. As the afternoon approached, all women who had lipsticks put some lipstick on their lips and their cheeks, and shared their lipsticks with those who had none. Even though it was hot, every woman got out her wrinkled dress and put it on so as not to show their skinny limbs. Men also wore their pants and shirts.

My mother wore a blue printed dress. She turned to me and asked, "Does it look good on me? Please, Bezio, put the lipstick on me, also on my cheeks. I don't have a daughter any more. You have to do it for me." I combed her hair and tried to make her look healthier.

Lotka, as much in pain as she was, looked cheerful with a red bow in her hair.

Jakob gave orders to scrub the toilet and the wooden floor. Every bunk bed should look neat. When Dr. Frommer arrives, everyone should be sitting on their bunks, not lying down or sleeping. Everyone listened to Jakob's orders.

That evening the bell rang twice. Immediately afterward I heard Ivan digging and lifting the cement plate. The cool air rushed into the bunker from the entrance across from my bunk.

The bunker was absolutely silent. Then I heard someone jumping into the bunker and the sound of dirt falling after the jump. A large head with black hair emerged, followed by a fat body. Dr. Frommer was breathing heavily. He entered the bunker and stood up, brushing the dirt from his dark suit.

Ivan followed him, carrying his medicine bag, smiling mischievously like a youngster.

Dr. Frommer looked around, cleared his throat, and said, "As you know, the only camp left is Jana. We are still a couple of hundred people left. Ivan has contacts in the camp, among them Engineer Backenroth. He approached me to come see you because some of you are sick. I took a big chance to get here, but I feel it is my duty to help those who are still alive in our town."

He then pushed himself through all along our bunk beds, stopping to talk and looking at all of us. Everyone was sitting, some smiling at him. He looked at the stove, the radio, and even touched the map that was hanging on the wall. "It's remarkable how this bunker was built," he said.

Jakob approached Dr. Frommer and told him, "I and the Schwartz family were the ones who conceived this bunker and built it along with Aron Shapiro. It took us three months to build. Now we are here over a year and, as you see, we are doing well."

Mrs. Schwartz couldn't wait to interject, "We spent all our money here and we worked hard. So we feel good, as you see. I cook and everyone has enough food."

Dr. Frommer sat down on the bunk right next to Lotka. He put his hand on her hair and patted her. "I know that you have a boil under your arm. May I see it? I will give you a salve that will help. You will feel good very soon."

Then he turned to Ivan and said, "The way I see all those who have been here for over a year, they look good. They don't look sick as you said."

He opened his medicine bag, took out the salve and some aspirins, and handed them to Lotka. She took them from him and asked, "You're not going to poison us, are you?"

He smiled at her. "Don't worry, my child, you all look good to me."

Ivan stood by without uttering a word. He had an embarrassed look on his face. As I watched him, I thought Ivan might be having regrets about his plan. To me, Ivan was a good young man, who took a chance to save our lives.

"Now it's time to go back, Ivan," Dr. Frommer told him. He closed his bag and handed it to Ivan. Then he pushed himself into the entrance and disappeared. A few minutes later I could hear the earth falling over the concrete cover. I looked at Lotka, who was smiling. Mrs. Schwartz hugged Recia. All of us took off our clothing, relieved to feel cooler again.

The Pig

August 3-4, 1944

The radio reports were telling us that the Russian armies were advancing on all fronts. We were especially interested in the southern front advancing toward Drohobycz. We were all anxious and exhausted. Everyone was on edge. For example, Mr. Galica, the dentist, was always at the radio. A stocky man who took up a lot of room, he seemed to surround the radio. Others resented him because he changed stations frequently and prevented them from reaching the radio. Mrs. Kupferberg lay very frail and exhausted, while Mr. Kupferberg screamed at his family, and Mike Kleiner insulted everyone he could.

The oldtimers had given all our money to Ivan for food and didn't have any money left. The newcomers had some money, but it wasn't enough to pay for all the food needed to feed 45 people. We had not eaten--or even seen--any meat during the entire sixteen months. We had been living almost entirely on barley and oats, so we figured that Ivan could still supply us for awhile. But time and money were running out.

Besides our shortage of money for food, we sensed that Ivan was tired of us. Because he had no new people coming in, he had no hope of seeing any more income from his enterprise. Ivan and his wife did not stay much at the house but spent most of their time in the village with their family. We listened intently to the news bulletins. The Russian army was approaching Tarnapol, a vital, strategic city in the offensive toward the Drohobycz area.

One Monday evening we heard footsteps above us. It was OK, we sighed with relief, because we recognized Ivan's steps. Within minutes he was digging the corner of the basement over the plate to open the bunker. Ivan's head appeared in the hole. Then he threw down something big wrapped in newspapers. He lowered himelf inside and with a mischievous smile on his face announced, "I got meat for you. You should eat it in good health." Ivan, whose face was red from sunburn, showed his white teeth in a big smile. "The Russians are coming. You will be out of here soon."

For the first time we were hopeful that we might live through this terrible 3 1/2 year experience. But still we could not take it for granted as long as there was even one German soldier in town.

After Ivan left and covered the entrance to the bunker, Mrs. Schwartz and Mrs. Bergwerk, our cooks, grabbed the bundle and unwrapped it swiftly. Their faces were all happy, smiling, excited at the prospect of cooking meat for a change instead of barley. But Mrs. Schwartz's smile changed to horror as she saw the quarter of pig she had just unwrapped. "No," she cried, dropping the pig meat on the floor. "We will not eat it!"

Mrs. Bergwerk by nature was a calm person. She looked at the chunk of meat with amazement. "It is *treif* [nonkosher]," she said, "and I will not eat it. But I will cook it. If anyone wants to eat it, it's OK with me."

When she said this, Mr. Schwartz, our holy man, jumped toward her. "If you cook this pig in the only pot we have, all the food cooked afterward will be *treif*. You are committing the biggest sin, forcing us all to eat *treif*!" Mr. Schwartz wagged his finger threateningly in Mrs. Bergwerk's face. "God will punish you forever and ever. Because if you eat this pig, we will not survive. This will be God's punishment."

A turmoil prevailed. Many of us were elated at the sight of meat, even pig meat, but many were very much against having this meat cooked. Most of us had not eaten pig meat ever. Mrs. Koenig, who had not kept a kosher home, raised her voice above the others, "We will eat the meat because we are hungry and God will forgive us."

Everyone argued loudly. Mike Kleiner, the horror man, forced his way through the crowd around the pig. "I *order* you to cook the pig," Mike shouted at Mrs. Schwartz and Mrs. Bergwerk. "You do what I say."

My mother said that if anyone wanted to eat the pig meat, he should. I felt the same way, and I was willing to eat it.

After a long exchange of insults and threats, Mr. Schwartz put on his *tallis* and began to pray for those poor souls who were going to commit the sin of eating pig meat.

Mrs. Koenig was smiling all along, saying to all, "I'm going to have the first good meal in a year and half." She enjoyed teasing Mr. Schwartz and all those who were against cooking the pig.

Finally, Mrs. Schwartz and Mrs. Bergwerk decided that they would cook the pig and those who wanted to could eat it. But it was late, and they decided to cook the meat the next day. Mrs. Bergwerk wrapped the meat back in the newspaper and put the bundle on the shelf by the stove.

The news that the Russians were approaching and only ten kilometers from us kept us awake, listening to the radio constantly. That night was the first time that newscasters mentioned that the armies were advancing toward Drohobycz.

Next morning our cooks washed the pig, added salt, and put it on the stove to cook. But most of us paid very little attention to the pig or to food in general. We were concerned with the Russian front and very fearful that something might go wrong in the last hours before our liberation.

As the pig bubbled in the big pot on the gas stove, suddenly our electricity and gas were cut off. It happened in the afternoon, the time when we usually slept. But no one was asleep that day because we were listening continuously to the radio. Suddenly the radio went dead and the lights went out, plunging us into the pitch-black darkness of an underground cave. We sat in the bunker in darkness until someone found and lit a flickering candle. Anxious voices filled the darkness-- What was going on? What would happen to us?

I realized then that we were in a peculiar situation without light and gas for cooking, not knowing what was happening outside.

The chunk of pig meat remained half raw in the pot on the stove. Mr. Schwartz had his wish--the pig would not be eaten by anyone.

Liberation

A year and a half of eating small portions of barley or oatmeal, and the heat and confinement of our bunker had caused a degeneration of both body and mind. We had lost all enthusiasm. I looked around and saw the Schwartzes, Kupferbergs, and my family. They were shadows in both mind and body.

My legs had become quite weak, and I had trouble walking even as far as the toilet. Alus, whose tall body lay on the bunk near me, was also very weak.

We kept the radio on all the time. Mundek switched the dial from German, to Polish, to Russian. The Russians were approaching our area, but the news bulletins were not precise about their armies' exact locations.

It was a time of complete exhaustion for me and for practically all of us oldtimers. We were resigned to whatever was going to happen to us, and a feeling of unreality prevailed. Liberation seemed an abstraction-- something distant, so long hoped for that we felt it would never come. Like a community of moles trapped below ground, we were part of an underground life with long-established habits. There was sort of a peculiar feeling about it all. It was very difficult for me to imagine the liberation.

After sixteen months of lying around in this hole, I wondered whether we would be able to walk, eat, and live a normal life. I couldn't think about it or even imagine it.

When Ivan brought us the quarter of a pig, he had opened the bunker for only a short while and closed it soon afterward. He was in a hurry to leave that night because the Russians were approaching. After he covered our entrance, we knew he left the house because we didn't hear him walking around upstairs.

He didn't talk to us much that night, not even to his two girlfriends. Ivan was a changed person. He was serious and nervous, and he didn't show much enthusiasm about his accomplishment. I really didn't know if he considered it an accomplishment to save forty-five Jews. He was doing his duty, but to whom? And he may not have felt comfortable with his family and friends about his secret. To hide Jews and save their lives was not very popular within the Ukrainian community, and Ivan was smart enough to realize it. Therefore, he left with his wife to go back to their village.

Jakob said joyfully, "We are being liberated, Bezio."

Mother, sitting next to me, had excitement and wonder in her voice, "I just can't believe it's true."

But nobody moved out of his bunk. Lying there, I listened for any noises or steps from upstairs. I hoped that Ivan would come and tell us what was happening outside. We needed to get out.

The hours went by. We had no food because we couldn't cook, and we didn't hear anything from Ivan. I felt that Ivan and his wife feared for their lives once their Ukrainian neighbors and family found out that they had saved Jews.

Now everyone was restless. The children cried, afraid of the darkness.

Then we heard Jakob's strong, confident voice. "Be quiet all. As it stands now, we really don't know what happens outside. Ivan is not upstairs, and night is approaching. Let's wait until morning. We hope that Ivan will be back, unearth us, and tell us what's going on outside. Let's not make any mistakes in the last minutes before liberation. We need to be cautious."

The candle was put out to save it for tomorrow. But nobody really slept. Everyone was talking, restless, and excited.

At 8 A.M. the next day Jakob lit the candle. We still were hoping to hear from Ivan, but he didn't come. We were entombed and needed to get out from the inside.

We could hear loud noises outside on the street. Our bunker shook from the heavy vehicles that were passing and the shells that were exploding around us. All of these noises were scaring us.

Mike Kleiner was getting angry and screaming. "Let's make some food," he commanded. "We can soak our oats in water."

Jakob spoke firmly, "Everyone who has any food must bring it forward so we can feed the children. We will wait until noon. If Ivan does not come to open the bunker, we will break out."

Everyone cried out to open the bunker. Among all the voices I heard, the loudest was Mr. Schwartz's. He was reciting the morning prayers by heart.

My thoughts went back to the days before the war, to my school days, my grandfather, my father, my brothers Szymon and Jakob, and my sister Clara. I remembered a Purim day when my mother baked a large challah with raisins and fresh *hamantashen* (tri-cornered cookies filled with prunes or poppy seeds) smelling of spices. My father and I came home from *shul*. We found the table covered with a white cloth, and the *challah* set on the table in front of my father's chair, so he could say the blessing. It was convenient to think of the past as I did during my entire stay in the bunker. Alus, lying next to me, would remind me daily of the foods we used to eat.

Now I watched the candle flickering on the stove, and I listened to the tumult around me.

August 5th, 4 P.M.

There was no sign of Ivan. Everyone was restless, especially the Shapiro brothers, who were physically stronger and emotionally hyper. They wanted to get out.

The oldtimers were weak, and the newcomers, our elite, including Mike Kleiner, were passive.

Yoske and Szymon Shapiro approached Jakob. "We can lift the cement plate from the inside," Szymon said eagerly. "I have an idea how to do it."

"Yes, it's time to go," Jakob replied. "We need to get into the house and see what the hell is going on outside."

Szymon told him his plan. "We are going to use the wood we have from the bunks to make a lever."

Szymon, Yoske, Manek Bergwerk, and Jakob were still the strongest among us, and they took on the task. They placed a long wooden plank vertically underneath the cement plate covering the entrance to the bunker. Then they took a large board and put one end of it under the vertical plank. This board extended horizontally into the bunker and was raised over a pile of wood two feet high. When three men stepped on the end of the plank in the bunker, it raised the other end beneath the cement plate. It pushed the vertical board upward and raised the cement plate, spilling earth inside the bunker. Then Manek, the smallest and strongest, crawled inside the entrance and lifted the plate from the inside. A lot of earth fell in, but the bunker was open at last.

Manek was the first to enter the cellar. Cautiously he went up the stairs and looked into the street through the kitchen curtains. He came down immediately and announced that he didn't see anyone on the street.

Immediately Jakob, I, and some others crawled out and went into the kitchen. We were very careful not to be seen from the outside. After a few minutes we saw two Red Army soldiers running up the street with machine guns in their hands.

It was a bright, sunny day. Now I noticed the inside of the kitchen. I looked out at the trees, flowers, and the shrubs. It was the first time I'd seen daylight in a year and a half, and the light dazzled my eyes. The sight of the two Red Army soldiers was the happiest sight in my life. It was unreal. Was it really possible that we were about to be liberated and that we would not die?

We stood at the window and behind the kitchen's glass door, waiting for other soldiers to pass by the house. We saw three more soldiers running up the street. At that moment Yoske, dressed only in his shorts and without a shirt, broke the glass door, pushed it open, and jumped out in front of them. "We are Jews!" Yoske screamed. "We are Jews! You liberated us!"

He ran to the soldier closest to him, knelt on the ground, and kissed the astonished soldier's dust-covered black army boots. Those of us who had come up from the bunker stepped out onto Ivan's front porch.

The soldiers were startled at first and pointed their guns at Yoske and at us. But right away they realized that we were no threat to them, so they lowered their guns.

A Russian officer came over to the porch and told us, "The Germans are still only a couple of kilometers from here behind the hill. We are clearing them out."

"Do you have water?" asked one of the soldiers.

Jakob ran into the bunker to bring a pot of drinking water for the soldiers.

We stood around and watched them drink. Jakob told them that forty-five Jews are in the house and asked the officer what we should do.

The officer replied, "You all get out of here because we haven't secured the area yet. We set up a command post down the street in an abandoned factory next to our artillery battery. You go there. A colonel is in charge. We've set up a kitchen for the night. They will take care of you, and in case we have to retreat, you'll be safe with us."

We all went down to the bunker to tell everyone to move out. Everyone, that is, but Yoske. He was so overcome with emotion, so excited, that he ran unclothed toward the Rynek, the city center, leaving all of us behind.

Jakob, my mother, and I got dressed inside the bunker. I put on my brother's navy striped suit and borrowed a pair of shoes from the Haberman boy, who owned both a pair of boots and a pair of shoes. My legs were still quite weak. Jakob and my mother had to help me as we walked slowly toward the Red Army command post. Many of the others followed us, including the Schwartz family.

But others remained in the bunker because they were not ready--either physically or mentally or both--to leave in a hurry. They were afraid to venture into the Russian military compound and wanted to stay safely inside the bunker until the area was secure.

It was already dusk when we arrived at the command post. At the entrance were four Red Army soldiers. About twenty of us halted right there. Jakob and I approached them, explaining that we are Jews and that the officer had told us that we could stay with them until the danger was over and then we would continue into town.

Inside were a couple of field desks, telephones, and chairs set up for the command post. About fifteen soldiers manned the telephones, keeping in touch with troops in the field. Otherwise, the place was empty. Again Jakob and I approached the colonel.

"We are Jews," I said. "We need shelter for overnight and some food."

The colonel looked at us and then turned to the soldiers nearest him. "Bring blankets for them all, and give them bread and meat."

"Thanks so much," I told him. "Where can we lie down?"

He answered with a smile, "This is the best hotel in town. Take all the room you need."

We found a corner, spread the blankets, and sat down. We ate the bread and meat the soldiers had given us. Food and freedom tasted delicious.

Throughout the night, Russian artillery batteries shelled the Germans. The voices of the soldiers who manned the telephones were music to my ears. It was the first time in more than three years that I felt safe, and the faces of my liberators looked like angels.

In the morning the colonel came over to us and said, "We chased those sons of bitches right into Hungary. You are safe now."

Within minutes the Russian soldiers gathered all their gear, folded it, put it onto trucks, and moved out to fight on.

My mother, Jakob, and I stood on Boryslawska Street, which led to the center of Drohobycz. It was the happiest and saddest moment in our lives. We were alive and free.

We walked slowly along Boryslawska Street past our house, the house where my grandfather and my aunts and cousins had lived. I saw the labor camp nearby. The street was quiet. People stayed indoors. Only a few stray dogs moved around.

Sadness overcame my mother, and she looked at Jakob and me. "Look, my sons, nobody remains. Why are we alive? Are we privileged? Why?"

I didn't answer her. I didn't know what to say.

We walked past a house where an elderly Polish couple lived. I noticed them working in their garden. I knew the man as the Cape Man because he always wore a cape. He knew my family. As we approached, he noticed us walking. He came over and said, "Mayer, you survived! How great! Where are you going?"

We stopped, and my mother told him, "We don't know. We are going to the Rynek to look for a place to live."

He looked at us from top to bottom. "Come stay with us until you find something," he said. "I have an extra

room. My wife will cook for you fresh vegetables. Please,
it is good for you."
    My mother thanked him, "It's fine. You are very kind.
Only for a day or two until we find an apartment."
    We stayed in his house for two days, eating three
meals a day. I basked in the sun each day and gained
strength.
    Then Jakob came to tell us that he had found an
apartment abandoned by Ukrainians or Germans who had
retreated with the German army. From empty apartments,
we gathered enough furniture for us to sleep and live.
    In the basement of our new apartment house, my
mother discovered a treasure: several sacks of potatoes! We
had what to eat, and mother made potato knishes, which I
sold every day to the Red Army soldiers who were passing
through Drohobycz. We earned enough money to buy some
used clothing and the shoes that I badly needed since I
walked around barefoot. Several days after we left the
bunker, the Haberman boy had asked for his shoes back.

    On June 29, 1941, the Jewish community of
Drohobycz numbered 17,000 men, women, and children.
At the liberation on August 5, 1944, only about 150 Jews
survived, all of them hidden in homes of various righteous
Gentiles. Among them were only two young children--
Mushka, who was four, and Anulcia, who was three and a
half. Both had survived in our bunker.

A few weeks later I was back in school, but none of my school friends were there.

Afterword

This is what happened to the survivors of our bunker after the war:

Mr. Schwartz, the holy man and one of the men who built the bunker, and **Mrs. Schwartz,** our cook, moved to Brazil with their three children. Mr. Schwartz worked for his brother in a pharmaceutical company.

Recia Schwartz, their daughter, who wrote poetry in the bunker, lived in Rio de Janeiro, Brazil, with her husband, a jewelry dealer.

Lotka Schwartz, who sang songs in the bunker, lived in Rio de Janeiro with her husband and two children.

Alus Schwartz, who lay next to me on the bunk and was one of the builders of the bunker, is a banker in Rio de Janeiro. He is married and has three children and several grandchildren.

Mr. and Mrs. Kupferberg moved to Israel, where they had a grocery store.

Mundek Kupferberg, who was our barber and in charge of the radio, lives in Israel, where he is a physician.

Bertha Kupferberg is married and is a pharmacist in Israel.

Rosa Bergwerk, our cook, moved to Brazil, where she remarried.

Manek Bergwerk, one of the builders of the bunker, was drafted by the Red Army right after liberation in 1944. He was killed in action in April 1945.

Mr. Hersh Ekstein, one of the builders of the bunker, was killed by robbers outside Drohobycz in January 1945.

Mrs. Rose Ekstein, his widow, left for Israel later. She remarried and moved to California.

Itzak Shoenfeld and **his two sisters** live in Israel. He is in the rope business, as he was before the war.

Fay and **Sala,** Itzak Shoenfeld's two girlfriends, left Poland for England. There they married their former boyfriends, and years later they moved to Israel.

Mr. and Mrs. Galica moved to Israel, where they practiced dentistry. He was a dentist, and she was his assistant.

The two children **Anulcia** and **Mushka** live in Israel. Both are married and have several children.

Mrs. Badjan, Mushka's mother, and **Grandma Badjan** live in Israel. Mrs. Badjan remarried; her husband was shot by the Germans before she entered our bunker.

The **Haberman family** moved to Israel. **Alex Haberman** is an engineer

Mike Kleiner, the horror man, was killed in Drohobycz when he fell off a truck in October 1944.

Yoske Shapiro, Aron's brother, was robbed and killed in May 1945 when he was on a business trip to Czechoslovakia.

Szymon Shapiro, Aron's other brother, and his sons **Beirel** and **Yankel** moved to the United States. The sons own a dental laboratory in Chicago.

No one knows what happened to **Mrs. Koenig,** who stole the two potatoes. None of us ever saw her again after she left the bunker.

Mr. Elie Heilig, who came to the bunker with the Shapiro family, found his sister and moved with her to Israel.

Mr. Paul Hertzig and his wife **Rose** moved to the United States. Their son became a prominent doctor in New York City.

Mr. Manek Zukerberg, the pharmacist, and his **wife** and **brother** and **sister-in-law** remained in Poland.

Genia, Ivan's girlfriend, eventually settled in New York City. She married a doctor and has children.

Mr. Landau, the last person to arrive in the bunker, eventually settled in Israel. He has a large family and became a partner in one of the largest ice cream factories in Israel.

Jakob Mayer, the organizer and leader of the bunker, moved to the United States in 1949. He owned a gift shop in New Jersey, married, and had two daughters.

Tonia Mayer, the main contact for building the bunker, came to the United States and married a businessman. She moved to Florida in 1980 to live near her son Bezio.

Bezio (Bernard) Mayer, the author, arrived in the United States in 1947 and received a B.S. degree from New York University and an M.S.W. degree from Barry University in Miami. He is a psychiatric social worker and lives in Florida. He has two sons.

And this is what happened to **Ivan Bur,** the Righteous Gentile, a Ukrainian who lived in the house during the entire time.

Ivan never returned to the house after the liberation. The last time I saw him was about a month after liberation. He was at the Red Army military induction center. When he saw me, he didn't acknowledge my presence, but kept on talking to his Ukrainian friends.

A few months later Mrs. Bur, who was pregnant, came to the marketplace, where my mother owned a small food store. She told my mother that she had been notified that Ivan was killed fighting the Germans near Berlin. My mother gave her food to take home with her.

Forty-nine years later, I went to Drohobycz and Stebnik, where the Burs used to live. I tried to find out what happened to Mrs. Bur and her child but I could not find anyone who knew of them.

Bernard, Mundek Kupferberg, and Alus Schwartz
nine months after the liberation.

Jakob, Tonia, and Bernard in Paris on way
to the United States in 1946.

Anulcia at the age of 3, before entering the bunker.

1992: Mushka, left, was four years old and Anulcia, who is an artist, was three when they were hiding in the bunker. They live in Israel and have children and grandchildren. Mushka and Anulcia were the only small children who survived in Drohobycz.

1992: Mrs. Janka Badjan, whose husband befriended
the Gestapo who later killed him in the forest. She is
the mother of Mushka and lives in Israel.

Israel 1992: Itzak Shoenfeld, 87, remembers:
"For 17 months I was hiding in fear of my life.
But I was comfortable to lie between the two
pretty girls."

1992: Lipcia Wegner, 82, was hidden in the
bunker for 18 months. She currently lives
in Israel.

Israel 1992: Alex Haberman, 66, with the model
of the bunker. He tells the "Entombed" story in
Israeli schools.

Drohobycz 1992: The Drohobycz courthouse where
the pogrom took place in July 1941. Over two hundred
Jews were killed.

Drohobycz 1992: The wall on Kowalska Street where the Jews were shot.

Drohobycz 1992: A monument on the wall
where the Jews were shot.

Drohobycz 1992: A monument over the mass grave
in Bronica. There are fourteen mass graves which
contain 14,000 Jews.

Drohobycz 1992: The Great Synagogue of Drohobycz;
it is now a furniture warehouse.

Drohobycz 1992: Inside the Great Synagogue

Drohobycz 1992: Statishe Werkstaten Labor Camp,
where I worked, is now a trade school. All 400 workers
perished in June 1943.

Drohobycz 1992: The coffee factory where my mother and I survived the first action by hiding under the sacks of grain.

Drohobycz 1992: My mother and I hid in this warehouse
during the second action on November 19, 1942.

Drohobycz 1992: The house where I spent wonderful years with my father, mother, brothers, and sister until 1937.

Drohobycz 1992: The house where I lived with sixteen
Jewish families in June 1941. All of them were taken
away and murdered.

Drohobycz 1992: The Drohobycz City Hall; there are no Jews currently living in Drohobycz.

Drohobycz 1992: The Drohobycz grade school where
I attended. It is approximately 100 years old.

Drohobycz 1992: Drohobycz Library as it was before the war.

Drohobycz 1992: The theatre in Drohobycz where
I attended many plays and concerts.